THE CONTROVE

Also in this series:

The Word for the World (John chapters 1–6)

The Crucified King (John chapters 15–21)
September 1996

The Controversial Christ

Growing with John's Gospel

Book 2: John chapters 7 – 14

Stephen Gaukroger
with Simon Fox

Crossway Books
Leicester

CROSSWAY BOOKS
38 De Montfort Street, Leicester LE1 7GP, England

First published 1996

British Library Cataloguing in Publication Data
A catalogue record for this book is available from the British Library.

ISBN 1-85684-139-1

Set in Baskerville

Typeset by Avocet Type, Brill, Aylesbury, Bucks.

Printed in Great Britain for Crossway Books
by Cox & Wyman Ltd, Reading, Berkshire.

CONTENTS

INTRODUCTION

John was one of the twelve disciples chosen by Jesus. So what we have in the Gospel of John is not an account written by some idle spectator who was not really involved in the events described. This gospel was not written by someone who turned up on the scene, rather like a journalist, asking people what happened and then reporting second-hand facts. John was actually there, seeing everything at first hand.

These days many people receive the teletext services on their televisions. It's remarkable how quickly the news stories are included on the news pages of Ceefax and Oracle. They enable you to keep right up to date with the news, twenty-four hours a day. But there is a small time-lag between the event happening and the report of it getting on to the teletext pages.

However, there is no time lag at all in John's Gospel. It wasn't that someone told someone who told someone who told someone who told John. He was actually there! He was called by Jesus to be one of the original proclaimers of the gospel. This is an eye-witness account from someone who walked with Jesus, talked with him, sat down to evening meals with him and chatted over the events of the day with him. John would have said to Jesus, 'What were you doing with that blind man this morning?' And Jesus would have answered, 'Well, I healed him, and I did it like this ... And when I've gone and the Holy Spirit comes you will be able to do the same thing, and it will happen like this ... and like this ...'

We all know that Jesus had twelve disciples. But John was not just one of the Twelve: he was one of the Three. The Three were Peter, James and John, the closest friends of Jesus. He had realized that he couldn't share himself fully with as many as twelve, so he chose three men out of the twelve to be his intimate confidants. In effect he was saying to them, 'I am going to share my life with you even more deeply, intimately and fully than with those other nine. I am going to share with you my principles of living, my principles of power.'

Chapter 9 of Mark's Gospel tells the story of the Transfiguration, in which Jesus takes these three men up a mountain, where they have an amazing experience: the glory of God descends upon Jesus, his clothes become dazzling white, and they see him somehow talking with Elijah and Moses, two of the Old Testament prophets. Only these three disciples had the privilege of seeing that great event, and John was one of them.

And not only was John one of the Three, but he was also the disciple who was closest to Jesus. In John 13:23 we read that at the Last Supper John, *the disciple whom Jesus loved, was reclining next to him.* In the ancient world people didn't eat at a table, sitting on chairs. Instead they ate lying down in a circle, leaning on one elbow. So John would have been lying next to Jesus, and they would have been able to talk about things quietly and intimately while they were eating together. Jesus shared some very important truths with John, his close friend, and John wrote them down for us so that we too can know Jesus personally.

Mark's Gospel was the first of the four gospels to be written. It is short, pithy and to the point; it has no long explanations. It is full of action and life. Then Matthew's Gospel was written especially for the Jews who needed a lot of explanations about Jesus. They knew all about Yahweh, the great God of the Old Testament, but who was this Jesus person? Then there was Luke's Gospel, which was written for the Gentiles, who had never heard of either Yahweh or Jesus and who needed a factual account of Jesus' life. That's why the story of his birth is fuller in Luke than in any other gospel. Luke was explaining to the Gentiles who Jesus was and where he came from. John's Gospel was the last to be written (perhaps at around AD 80), and it was an attempt to say to the world, 'This is what Jesus means.' It is a gospel of explanation, a gospel of purpose. There are only eight miracles recorded in John, while there are dozens in the other gospels. John isolates each miracle and makes a point out of it and says, 'This is who Jesus is, this is why he came into the world.'

If you are not yet a Christian or have only recently become one, there is no better place to begin learning about Jesus than in John's Gospel. Even if you have been a Christian for decades, there are truths in this gospel which will amaze you.

Chapter 1

We are a pilgrim people

After this, Jesus went around in Galilee, purposely staying away from Judea because the Jews there were waiting to take his life. But when the Jewish Feast of Tabernacles was near, Jesus' brothers said to him, 'You ought to leave here and go to Judea, so that your disciples may see the miracles you do. No-one who wants to become a public figure acts in secret. Since you are doing these things, show yourself to the world.' For even his own brothers did not believe in him.

Therefore Jesus told them, 'The right time for me has not yet come; for you any time is right. The world cannot hate you, but it hates me because I testify that what it does is evil. You go to the Feast. I am not yet going up to this Feast, because for me the right time has not yet come.' Having said this, he stayed in Galilee.

(John 7:1–9)

What was the Feast of Tabernacles? It was a Jewish celebration (about mid October) to remind the people that at one time they had lived in the wilderness, travelling from Egypt to the Promised Land. At that time they had been constantly on the move and God had provided for all their needs. During the Feast of Tabernacles the people built simple shacks or tents which represented the mobile, temporary homes they had lived in during the wilderness days. During the Feast the people would live in these for a day or two, and the more devout Jews would live in them for a week or so. During the wilderness years they had been a pilgrim people and the Feast was meant to remind them that they were still a pilgrim people. God was saying to them through the Feast that they were not to put their trust in houses and buildings and possessions; their relationship with him was the most valuable thing they had. Their homes might seem permanent, but in reality they were temporary: the only permanent thing they had was their relationship with their God.

In the Feast of Tabernacles God was saying, 'Permanence is found only in me.' God was reminding them of the slavery from which he had delivered them; of the nomadic, tent-dwelling existence they had known in the wilderness; and that then even his temple had been a movable tent. Later he had allowed them to have a permanent temple in Jerusalem, but they were not meant to rely even on that: they were to rely only on God himself.

Perhaps today we Christians would benefit from celebrating a kind of Feast of Tabernacles. We need to be reminded, as the Jews did, that our homes and possessions are merely temporary things compared to our relationship with God. Of course, this truth cuts right across the message which the culture around us is constantly communicating to us. The mass media, and television in particular, tell us that material possessions are permanent and important. But the truth is that all the things we own, and our careers and money and status are merely temporary. In one hundred years' time everything we own will be dust as far as we are concerned. Our modern homes will probably have been demolished, all our prized possessions may be so much rubbish, rusting and disintegrating, buried deep in a refuse tip somewhere. By contrast, the work of the Holy

Spirit in our lives is of permanent, eternal significance.

We may say that Jesus is the Lord of our lives, but are we really living as if only our relationship with him is of lasting importance? Or are we at least partially being brainwashed by the message of the world around us? Are we concerned about 'getting on' and fulfilling the expectations which society has of us? If we don't see the things of the world for what they are – fleeting, ephemeral things of no lasting value – we will always be half-hearted in our commitment to Jesus, because the other half of our hearts will be committed to the pursuit of wealth, success, status and all the other rubbish which the world believes to be important. Are we building our lives on sand, which will surely slip through our fingers, or are we building upon Jesus the Rock? Naked we came into the world, and naked we will go out of it. We cannot take anything with us into eternity except our relationship with Jesus. The only thing that is going to last for ever is God and ourselves in relationship with him.

God's perfect timing

Sometimes in John's Gospel when Jesus talks about time he means the inescapable hour that cannot be altered a point on the future calendar. He says, 'the hour is coming …' and then makes some great statements about his forthcoming crucifixion and resurrection (for instance John 12:23, Greek *hora,* NIV *hour*). He knows that this is an essential part of his ministry as the Messiah: he knows that hour is coming, he cannot avoid it and he does not want to avoid it, because he wants to obey his Father. That hour is part of God's plan for him, and it is a plan which cannot be changed.

In other instances Jesus talks about time in a different way, as he does in the passage above. Here he is not talking about a fixed point in time to which he is inevitably moving but rather a window of opportunity

(Greek *kairos,* NIV *time*). He says,'*The right time for me has not yet come*' (verse 6): in other words, 'Now is not the right time for me to be publicly revealed as the Messiah. That opportunity will surely come, but it has not come yet.'

We can see that Jesus possessed a remarkable inner peace throughout his life, despite all the momentous things which he was doing and which were happening to him and around him. I believe that the secret of his peace was his sense of God's timing. He always knew when to act and when not to act in a certain way. There were many times in his life when people tried to push him into doing things which they thought were right – for example, his brothers told him that he should go to Judea and make a name for himself as a 'public figure'. Yet Jesus resisted these pressures because he had a clear sense of God's timing. He knew when it was right to go ahead and when it was right to hang back. He had an abiding sense that his Father was in control of his life and would not let events happen too quickly or too slowly; he knew that God's timing was always perfect. He was sensitive to that timing; he didn't try to rush God or hold back from God's purposes.

In the Garden of Gethsemane he prayed,

> *'My Father, if it is possible, may this cup be taken from me.'*
> (Matthew 26:39)

He knew that the terrible agony of the cross awaited him, and yet he submitted to God's will: *'Yet not as I will, but as you will'* (verse 39). He knew that the time was right for him to lay down his life as a sacrifice for our sin. He was saying to God, 'I know what you want me to do, Father, and although the human part of me shrinks from the suffering I must endure, I know I must go ahead and lay down my life. My time has now come.'

Often we Christians today live frantic, frenetic, pressurized lives, because we are not aware of the timing of God. We want to dictate to God when things should happen or when we should do things. It is tempting to pray: 'Lord give me patience – and give it to me *now!*' Often we want to rush ahead of God, thinking that God is moving too slowly. But he is always moving at exactly the right speed. Sometimes we are desperately anxious to get on with things, and God says, 'Did I tell you to do that?' Foolishly we think we can accomplish something even if God doesn't want it to be done at that particular time. The fact is that we will achieve nothing of lasting worth unless we wait for God's timing. Scripture says that

With the Lord a day is like a thousand years, and a thousand years are like a day.

(2 Peter 3:8)

Whenever we lag behind what God wants us to do, we will feel pressure; and whenever we try to rush ahead of God we will step out of what he has in mind. So knowing that God's timing is perfect should give us a sense of relaxation. We do not need to be pressurized: we can relax in the knowledge that God knows what he is doing and will achieve his purposes in the right way at the right time.

Waiting for God does not of course mean we have to be idle and just waste our time; it means waiting in the sense of resting in God, knowing that his perfect time will come and he will then work out his great purposes. To know the peace which Jesus knew we need to rest in the timing of God. This is not easy, especially if we are young and active, but it gets easier with practice. If we decide that such peace is beyond us and never ask for it we shall, of course, never achieve it.

A double-edged sword

Among the crowds there was widespread whispering about

him. Some said, 'He is a good man.' Others replied, 'No, he deceives the people.'

(John 7:12)

We come across the phenomenon frequently in John's Gospel. Jesus always provokes a mixed response. Some people react positively to him, others react negatively. Every time Jesus says something publicly or does a miracle or some other act, it divides the people. This is still true today; he is the controversial Christ. Whenever the word of God is proclaimed there will be a mixed response. Some people will accept it and others will reject it.

Verse 13 says, *But no-one would say anything publicly about him for fear of the Jews.* So people were muttering and whispering about Jesus in small groups; nobody would confess out loud their faith in him as the Messiah, because they were afraid of what the Jewish religious hierarchy would do to them. Fear of other people dominated their thinking and behaviour. The same is true for many Christians today. Some of us live under a tremendous fear of people and we need to be liberated from it. Often we are frightened to say what we believe because we are worried about what the response of other people will be. That is the case both outside the church and inside it: we often fail to speak frankly to our fellow Christians, and we fail to be effective witnesses to those outside the body of Christ. God wants us not to be afraid of what people will say; he wants us to be so filled with his Holy Spirit that we will speak lovingly, wisely, clearly and boldly about Jesus.

The people who were whispering about Jesus were too afraid to confess that he was the Christ. That is the pressure which we have to face. If we merely say that Jesus was a great moral teacher and a good man – someone who is a worthy subject for a film or a play –

then people will be quite happy with that and no-one will be offended by what we say. But if we start saying that Jesus is the Christ, the Lamb of God who died for our sins, then people will get upset. If we say that Jesus is the Son of God and that there is no way to God except through him, people will get hot under the collar. People do not like being confronted with the full truth about Jesus, because they then have to make a decision about him: they must either accept him as their Saviour or reject him.

Today we are living in a culture in which the uniqueness of Jesus is constantly denied. People are very happy to say that Jesus was a wonderful man and are keen to include him in their Top Ten of great spiritual and moral leaders, along with Mahatma Gandhi, Martin Luther King, Mother Teresa, Saint Francis, the Buddha, Muhammad, Confucius, Socrates and others. People are quite happy to venerate Jesus as one holy person among many, but they object when we say that in fact Jesus is in a completely different category from any other spiritual leader, because he is the one and only Son of God, sent from God to be our only Saviour and Lord. And because we know that people will object to this, we are afraid to speak out the truth. Hebrews 4:12 says the Word of God is *Sharper than any double-edged sword*: it inevitably divides people, provoking a mixed response. The Holy Spirit wants to release us from our fear of people and to empower us to speak boldly for God.

Chapter 2

Learning from the Father

Not until halfway through the Feast did Jesus go up to the temple courts and begin to teach. The Jews were amazed and asked, 'How did this man get such learning without having studied?'

Jesus answered, 'My teaching is not my own. It comes from him who sent me. If anyone chooses to do God's will, he will find out whether my teaching comes from God or whether I speak on my own …'

(John 7:14–17)

Jesus was saying to the Jews, 'No, I didn't go to Jerusalem University. No, I haven't studied formally like the Scribes and the Pharisees; I have learned not from human teachers but directly from my heavenly Father. My teaching and preaching is based not on academic qualifications; it has the authority of God himself.' Matthew records that after Jesus had finished preaching the Sermon on the Mount,

the crowds were amazed at his teaching, because he taught as one who had authority, and not as their teachers of the law.

(Matthew 7:28–29)

Jesus received his education through having a personal relationship with his Father in heaven: the Father shared his truth with Jesus and Jesus passed that truth on to the people.

This has important implications for us today. Now, of

course, academic education is very valuable and important: if God has given someone a sharp, powerful mind, that is something to be thankful about. The church needs thinkers – people who can wrestle with difficult concepts and communicate the gospel to an educated audience. We should never underestimate the value of a mind which is surrendered to God: the Lord will use that person's mind for his glory. However, there is something more important than mere intelligence. The education that really matters is the spiritual education which comes from God through having a personal relationship with him. If we will regularly read the Word of God and pray and develop our relationship with the Father, he will teach us, and as a result of this what we say about Jesus will have divine authority. Whether we possess a whole string of degrees or whether we failed to get any academic qualifications at all at school, we can all be educated by God and we can all speak with his authority.

Often I have heard Christians say things like, 'I'm not very bright – I can't understand all this theology and doctrine. I can't talk to people about Jesus. What if someone asks me a difficult question? I'll look stupid!' Really we have no excuse to say things like that. We are all capable of being educated in this spiritual sense; through walking with God faithfully in our lives, we can be educated by God's Spirit, and we can speak about Jesus with God's power and authority. Being intelligent is not essential. I'm sure most of us must have heard talks and sermons by highly educated speakers, and the message was very learned and clever, but it was as dry as dust because it was just human knowledge and lacked the anointing of the Holy Spirit. Of course, education and cleverness are useful and helpful if it is given over to God's service, but it is not essential. We need to reject utterly the faithless, negative attitude which says, 'I'm useless, I can't do it, I can't cope, I'm not very bright, I've got nothing to offer people.' What we have to offer is what we have been given by God, neither more nor less. I studied at Spurgeon's College for four years, but when I preach, it makes an impact on people not because I have read a lot of theology books, but because it is anointed by God. If my preaching has a lasting influence on people, it has that influence because it has God's authority and power in it. I can only give out through preaching what I have first received from God. Only God's living truth will last into eternity as it changes people's lives.

The apostle Paul was an academic who sat at the feet of the great Jewish teacher Gamaliel, and yet he needed to be converted and to learn from God. Jesus had no academic education but instead sat at the feet of the Father and learned the wonderful gospel message from him. We today can all do the same: we can all sit at the feet of the greatest Teacher in the universe. Our guidebook, the Bible, is easily available, our experience of life with our teacher goes on with every breath we draw and he is available for consultation twenty-four hours a day. The education which he gives us will have eternal value.

Judging by appearances

Jesus said to the people,

'Has not Moses given you the law? Yet not one of you keeps the law. Why are you trying to kill me?' 'You are demon-possessed,' the crowd answered. 'Who is trying to kill you?' ... Jesus said, to them ... 'Stop judging by mere appearances and make a right judgment.'

(John 7:19–21, 24)

Jesus knew that the Jewish religious leaders were trying to kill him. They wanted to get rid of him because they saw him as a trouble-maker, a rabble-rouser and a preacher of heresy. However, the ordinary Jews had no idea of what was going on in the higher echelons of their society: they didn't understand the power politics, the plotting, the intrigue. When Jesus said to the crowd, *'Why are you trying to kill me?'* he was speaking not to them but to the religious leaders. The people in the crowd thought he must be crazy to think that someone was trying to kill him, because they were ignorant of what was going on in the background. They didn't know the true facts of the situation: they saw that Jesus had apparently been left alone by the authorities, so they supposed he was merely imagining the plot to kill him. They had made a wrong conclusion based on inadequate information. That was why Jesus said to them, *'Stop judging by mere appearances, and make a right judgment.'*

Time after time in the ministry of Jesus we see people making wrong judgments based on mere appearances. Jesus does something or says something, and immediately people get hold of the wrong end of the stick: they make a judgment which is too quick and superficial. They have not thought the issue through and don't know the facts in the background. Jesus had to live with continual misunderstanding. Both his disciples and the crowds kept on misunderstanding him. So Jesus says to them, 'Stop judging by mere appearances – there is more to this than meets the eye.'

I believe that Jesus still wants to say this to us today. Too often we make superficial judgments about people without knowing the full facts. More times than I care to recall church members have come to my study or phoned me up, worried or upset about what So-and-So was supposed to have said or done, when they didn't really know the facts and hadn't bothered to find out what they were. Many times I have brought the two parties concerned together and got each of them to tell their side of the story, and usually the whole controversy turns out to be based on a misunderstanding and ignorance of the facts. And yet the people never bothered to find out the facts, and had not been on speaking terms for a month, and great damage had been done to the fellowship as a result. Too often people respond emotionally and hastily, just like the crowd did here. Too often we respond carnally and immaturely and unspiritually, without letting the Spirit of God tell us how we ought to respond in the situation.

We all need to take Jesus' words very seriously: *Stop judging by mere appearances, and make a right judgment* – a judgment based on facts, not gossip, on spiritual maturity, not emotion. Jesus wants us to be deep-thinking, serious-minded people of God who judge things carefully and weigh up the evidence and seek to discover the facts before responding to a situation, who try to find out what has really happened and why it happened before making any sort of pronouncement or decision. We must stop jumping to conclusions, we must stop judging other Christians without knowing what the situation really is. By our hasty, superficial reactions we do a great deal of damage to the body of Christ. We need to repent of the hurt we have caused other people by our hastiness.

Pointing the finger

Jesus said to them, 'I did one miracle, and you are all astonished. Yet, because Moses gave you circumcision … you circumcise a child on the Sabbath. Now if a child can be circumcised on the Sabbath so that the law of Moses may not be broken, why are you angry with me for healing the whole man on the Sabbath?'

(John 7:21–23)

The people were criticizing Jesus because he healed someone on the Sabbath, when no work of any kind was meant to be done. They saw Jesus' healing someone on the Sabbath as a transgression of the Law. But

Jesus responds by showing the people that they themselves do not keep the Law consistently. It was part of the Law that a male child had to be circumcised on the eighth day after his birth, and sometimes that eighth day would be a Sabbath day. Despite the Sabbath ban on work, the child would still be circumcised if the eighth day were a Sabbath. So this too was technically a breaking of the Law, where one part of the Law seemed to come into conflict with another part. Jesus then argued,

'Now if a child can be circumcised on the Sabbath so that the law of Moses may not be broken, why are you angry with me for healing the whole man on the Sabbath?'

In other words, 'Are you telling me that it's all right to operate on a child's body on the Sabbath but it's not all right to make someone's body whole on the Sabbath? If you can make exceptions to the letter of the Law, why can't I?' He showed them their own inconsistency and hypocrisy.

This was an example of the sort of technical knots which the Jews of Jesus' time had become tied up in. God had given them the Law as a guideline for their behaviour, but the Scribes and Pharisees had turned it into a rigid, legalistic system which put people into bondage and took away their freedom. The Law had been designed by God to protect the children of Israel from excess, from God's anger, from the diseases and disasters that were the result of ungodliness, but the religious leaders had made the protective Law into a source of pain and torment to the people. Jesus clearly exposed what they had done, and moreover the falsity of their position, because although they insisted on strict observance of the Law, they had invented all sorts of loopholes and exceptions.

We need to be careful that we do not find ourselves falling into the trap of hypocrisy and inconsistency, of pointing the finger accusingly at others. It is often the case that we are most critical of the sins in others of which we ourselves are guilty or which we are sorely tempted to commit. For example, people who complain about other people being gossips are often gossips themselves or are tempted to gossip. They see that sin in other people, and they can feel the temptation to follow suit bubbling up in themselves, and so they are afraid of that sin, lest they themselves become guilty of it. Sometimes the people who are self-appointed moral watchdogs over other people's lives have unrighteousness and inconsistency at the heart of their own lives. Such people insist on others following the moral rules which they see as crucial, but the rules are for other people, not for themselves. There is a tendency to expect other people to live up to standards which we ourselves fail to achieve. We may criticize people for committing a particular sin, and yet we ourselves may be committing the same sin in a different situation. This sort of inconsistency and hypocrisy is very common in the church and it displeases God. This is another area of our lives where we need to repent and receive God's forgiveness.

Jesus the Living Water

On the last and greatest day of the Feast, Jesus stood and said in a loud voice, 'If anyone is thirsty, let him come to me and drink. Whoever believes in me, as the Scripture has said, streams of living water will flow from within him.' By this he meant the Spirit, whom those who believed in him were later to receive.

(John 7:37–39)

On the last day of the Feast of Tabernacles the custom was that a priest would be sent down from the temple to the Pool of Siloam and would gather up a small quantity of water (about two pints). He would bring it back to the temple courtyard, where there would be great crowds of worshippers praising God in the words of Psalms 113 and 119. There the water would be poured out as a symbol of the water which God provided for the people during the wanderings in the wilderness and which he still provided for them. During the wilderness years God always provided water – sometimes through a miracle, sometimes by means of a freshwater spring. The people always had water, despite the fact that they were in a desert.

This was the context in which Jesus made his amazing statement, *'If anyone is thirsty, let him come to me and drink.'* Jesus had a keen sense of the dramatic, and he used the last day of the Feast as a powerful visual aid to get his message across. In effect he was saying, 'I am the Living Water. I am the real, spiritual water for your souls to drink. Today you are celebrating the fact that God provided water during the wilderness years, and that he still provides water today for your crops. God provides water for you, and water is life. But I am the Life, the river of life, and if you believe in me you will have a well of this living water rushing up from within you and flowing out of you to others. That is the kind of water you really need. You need my Holy Spirit within you.' Jesus is still saying the same thing to us today. If we will welcome him into our lives as our Saviour and Lord, he will satisfy our spiritual thirst with his living water, with his presence in our lives.

Spiritual blinkers

Finally the temple guards went back to the chief priests and Pharisees, who asked them, 'Why didn't you bring him in?'

'No-one ever spoke the way this man does,' the guards declared.

'You mean he has deceived you also?' the Pharisees retorted. 'Has any of the rulers or of the Pharisees believed in him? No!

But this mob that knows nothing of the law—there is a curse on them.'

(John 7:45–49)

These verses show us very clearly that the Jewish leadership were suffering from a case of incurable unbelief. They had simply closed their minds and their eyes to who Jesus might be. They were spiritually blind, so they could not see that Jesus really was the Messiah. Their minds and spirits were full of a dense fog which prevented them from seeing the truth which was right beneath their noses. If one objectively considers the amazing miracles which Jesus did, his authoritative, God-empowered teaching and his wonderful, unique personality, it is blatantly obvious that he was the Son of God. And yet the Scribes and Pharisees just could not see it, because they did not want to see it. They had their legalistic blinkers on and they were unwilling to take them off, and so they could not see Jesus' true identity.

In verse 50 we encounter Nicodemus once again. By this time he was probably a secret believer in Jesus, but because he was still a member of the Sanhedrin he could not make his faith public. He tried to stick up for Jesus, saying:

'Does our law condemn a man without first hearing him to find out what he is doing?'

(verse 51)

I suspect that he wanted Jesus to speak to the Sanhedrin, so that they could all hear the things he had heard when he went to see Jesus secretly at night. He probably hoped that the authority of Jesus' message would bowl the Sanhedrin over and convince them that Jesus really was the Messiah. But they dismissed his suggestion out of hand – they were unwilling to listen to what Jesus had to say. Their reply to Nicodemus was,

'Are you from Galilee too? ... a prophet does not come out of Galilee!'

(verse 52)

Sometimes today we can be spiritually blind. God is saying something clear to us, and yet we can't see it: it is obvious, and yet it seems obscure and difficult to us. Sometimes we get a bee in our bonnet and we get so locked into some particular approach to things that we become totally deaf to what God wants to say to us. In other words we cannot see God because of the blinkers which impair our vision. God wants us to take those blinkers off and open our eyes to the bright sunshine of his presence; he is saying to us, 'I am here in your life, I am real, I am alive. I have things I want to say to you – things you have been avoiding for weeks or months or years. Avoid them no longer. Come to me and know my power and don't be unbelieving any more.' He wants us to reject the spirit of unbelief within us, to rebuke it and to open our eyes to all that he has for us. Jesus says to us, 'Don't be like the Jewish religious leaders. Be men and women who are truly mine, with eyes open to see me and ears open to listen to my Word.'

Chapter 3

The mercy of Jesus

> *The teachers of the law and the Pharisees brought in a woman caught in adultery. They made her stand before the group and said to Jesus, 'Teacher, this woman was caught in the act of adultery. In the Law Moses commanded us to stone such women. Now what do you say?' They were using this question as a trap, in order to have a basis for accusing him.*
>
> (John 8:3–6)

In the NIV translation there is a little bracket at the end of chapter 7 which says, 'the earliest and most reliable manuscripts do not have John 7:53 – 8:11'. Our English New Testaments are translations from the Greek in which the books were originally written, and these translations are based on numerous manuscripts and fragments of manuscripts, some of which were written down soon after Jesus' lifetime and others a hundred years or so after his death. And the most reliable of these manuscripts do not have the passage which appears in our Bibles as John 7:53 – 8:11. This is very unusual in the New Testament; in fact there is only one other case where an entire passage is in doubt, and that is at the end of Mark's Gospel.

However, this does not mean that we must dismiss this passage as being unscriptural. Most scholars are agreed that the incident with the woman caught in adultery actually happened. In fact not long after Jesus' time there was a Christian preacher called Papias who knew about this story and often preached on it. So the passage records an actual historical event; the question is, should it be here in John's Gospel, or should it be somewhere else – after Luke chapter 21, for example? We are not certain whether John himself wrote the passage or whether a later editor, knowing it to be an important incident in Jesus' ministry, thought it should be included and inserted it here. This slight confusion does not mean that we should reject the passage; we can still accept and believe it as part of the Bible.

Having sorted all that out, let's now look at the passage itself. Jesus was presented with a dilemma. Here was a woman who had been caught in adultery. The tense of the Greek verb here means that she was actually engaged in adulterous sexual intercourse when she was caught, so there is no doubt that she was guilty of sexual sin. It was a cut-and-dried case: she was without doubt an adulteress. And so they brought this woman to Jesus in order to trap him.

We might well ask, what about the man in the case? It takes two to commit adultery. It was typical of the blinkered hypocrisy of the Jewish leaders that they allowed the man to go free (some have even conjectured that he was one of them!). Such double standards are not unheard of today, even, or especially, in our churches.

This was the dilemma. The Old Testament Law said that a woman caught in adultery ought to be stoned to death. (However, even in the Law there was a caveat to the effect that mercy could be shown in such situations, so that stoning for adultery was in fact a punishment which was rarely inflicted.) Jesus knew that he would fall into their trap if he said 'No, she should not be stoned,' because they would then be able to say, 'So you think God's Law can be disregarded? That invalidates all of your teaching!' But if Jesus were to say 'Yes,' then the teachers and Pharisees would have an excuse to go to the Roman authorities and report Jesus. The Romans had reserved for themselves the right to decide all matters of life and death: the Jewish rulers were allowed to administer justice in more minor matters, but deciding whether or not to put someone to death was the sole prerogative of the Romans. So if Jesus were to say, 'Yes, she should be stoned,' he would in effect be usurping the Romans' authority over the death penalty.

Jesus saw right through their obnoxious little trick and gave them no answer, merely bending down and writing on the ground with his finger. It would be very interesting to know what he wrote! He was probably just doodling, mulling the matter over, determined not to be trapped by their sneaky questions. But they kept on nagging him, so eventually he straightened up and said to them,

'If any one of you is without sin, let him be the first to throw a stone at her.'

(verse 7)

In other words he was saying, 'you have the right to stone her only if you yourselves are sinless.' And so, shamed and embarrassed and outwitted by Jesus' answer, one by one the woman's accusers sidled away. Once again Jesus had exposed their hypocrisy.

The big issue here is the difference between the religious leaders' attitude to the woman and Jesus' attitude to her. They were just using her as a device to trap Jesus: they couldn't care less what happened to her – they wouldn't have cared if she had been stoned to death. Her life or death was of no significance to them; she was just a tool, a victim. But Jesus cared about the woman: that was why he showed mercy towards her. Yes, she was an adulteress. Jesus did not try to pretend she was innocent but he was unwilling to see her put to death for her sin. He expressed God's mercy towards her. Yes, she had sinned, she had broken the Law, but Jesus forgave her.

Jesus never tolerated hypocrisy. He cut through it with the razor-sharp edge of his tongue. He never used his tongue to hurt people just for the sake of it, as we sometimes do, but when confronted with hypocrisy he would cut right through it with his authoritative words and expose the heart of the matter. The religious people of his day who were so quick to condemn others for their sins were themselves full of sin and corruption. Jesus often called the Pharisees hypocrites, and he also called them 'whited sepulchres' – that is, tombs which were white, clean and beautiful on the outside, but on the inside were full of corruption and the stench of old, rotting bones.

The danger of hypocrisy

Hypocrisy did not die out in Jesus' time; there is still a great deal of hypocrisy in the church today. Some Christians, or rather people who call themselves Christians, are puffed up with their knowledge of Scripture and know what the Bible says about any given subject; they consider themselves to be mature, wise, knowledgeable Christians. But despite this their personalities are warped by sin and selfishness; their family life, their personal morality, their business ethics, their behaviour at work – all of these things stink because there is rampant hypocrisy in their lives. And we should be careful that we do not point the finger at others and accuse them of hypocrisy: we should have the humility to ask ourselves whether there is hypocrisy in our own lives too. Is the way we live completely consistent with what we believe? Do we really practise what we preach? Or are we spiritual and holy on the outside but full of sin and compromise on the inside? Jesus hates hypocrisy: it angers him when we profess to be Christians with our mouths but our behaviour is sub-Christian. We find it so easy to point an accusing finger at others, but Jesus points his finger back at us and exposes our own hypocrisy. How dare we draw attention to the sins of others when we ourselves are sinful – often committing the very same sins we are condemning in others!

Jesus is angry with our double standards, and yet we need to remember that if we repent of our sins he will always be merciful to us, as he was to the woman in this story. Jesus has already taken upon himself the punishment for our sins by dying for us on the cross, and now he longs to be merciful to us if we will repent.

Augustine, one of the early Church Fathers, believed that this passage was originally in John's Gospel but was dropped from it later because it gave the impression that Jesus thought that adultery was not a sin that mattered. But I fail to see how anyone could interpret the passage that way, because of what Jesus says at the very end of it. Once the woman's accusers had gone away Jesus asked her,

'Woman, where are they? Has no-one condemned you?' 'No-one sir,' she said. 'Then neither do I condemn you,' Jesus declared. 'Go now and leave your life of sin.'

He did not merely say to the woman, *'neither do I condemn you'*; he also said, *'Go now and leave your life of sin.'* That little sentence is crucial. Jesus was saying to her, 'From this point on, stop sinning.' Jesus is no soft touch when it comes to sin. He is not a white-haired old grandfather who looks down benignly from heaven saying, 'It's okay' – you just go ahead and sin. I really don't mind too much.' Jesus is not like that. He will not tolerate sin. Having forgiven the adulterous woman of her sin, he expected her to try to live the rest of her life in a godly manner. He was saying to her, 'I have forgiven you for your sin of adultery, but don't do it again.'

The scope of Jesus' mercy

It is true that Jesus is merciful. He will forgive any sin we repent of, no matter how awful it is. He will forgive us for murdering someone, for raping someone, for inflicting grievous bodily harm on someone. He will forgive us for a lifestyle of theft and crime. He will forgive us pride, selfishness, cheating people out of money, manipulating and blackmailing people emotionally, hurting people in all sorts of ways. If we will come to Jesus in repentance, there is no sin we have committed which is too awful for him to forgive. Jesus not only saves to the uttermost; he also saves from the guttermost. He can get down below where we are and lift us up. There is no-one who is so bad that they are beyond the love and mercy of God. No matter how far gone someone is in their sin, it is never too far for Jesus to reach and bring them to himself. We need to believe in Jesus' eagerness to forgive us; we need to feel the joy of our forgiveness. It is very exciting and refreshing and liberating to know that we are fully forgiven by God through Jesus.

But the fact that God is willing to forgive does not mean that he does not take sin seriously. He does not gloss over our sin, ignoring it and saying, 'It doesn't really matter.' On the contrary, our sin is so serious and dreadful that God had to send his only-begotten Son, Jesus, to die a bloody and brutal death on a cross for us; on that cross Jesus took the punishment which was rightfully ours so that we would not have to suffer it and could instead have forgiveness and new life in Jesus.

Sometimes our attitude to repentance and forgiveness is far too casual. We come to God and say sorry for a particular sin, but we aren't really sorry enough, and so we commit the sin again the next day. We become stuck on a kind of merry-go-round of sin: sinning, repenting, sinning, repenting ... In order to stop committing the sin an act of the will is required. We must sincerely resolve in our hearts not to commit this sin any more; unless we make this decision, nothing is going to change; we will keep on committing the sin. Of course we shall need more than willpower. The strength of God's Holy Spirit will be necessary to break a really ingrained habit. But we shall get nowhere if we merely 'let go and let God' as the popular saying has it. We need to cooperate fully with him, not just passively, but genuinely wanting to change and being determined about it.

Chapter 4

Judging by human standards

> *When Jesus spoke again to the people, he said, 'I am the light of the world. Whoever follows me will never walk in darkness, but will have the light of life.'*
>
> (John 8:12)

After the incident of the woman caught in adultery, which interrupted the account of Jesus' debate with the Jewish leaders at the Festival, we rejoin the action at verse 12. At this point Jesus made a staggering claim, *'I am the light of the world'* not *a* light *in* the world, but '*the* light *of* the world'. At a given moment at the end of the Feast the great candelabra were lit in the Court of the Women. The brilliancy of that light cast everything else into shadow; beyond its rays people stumbled about the streets, but whoever came near could see where he or she was going. It was a dramatic moment for Jesus to claim to be the light of the world!

The lights represented for the Jews the great pillar of fire which had accompanied the returning Israelites across the desert with Moses. It was like the presence of God. Jesus was identifying himself with that light.

If you go back to the beginning of the gospel (1:1–4) you will recall that John had no doubt about who the *light of the world* was – God in human form, the word made flesh. He was the *light of men.* Whatever Jesus' hearers understood on that evening at the Feast John leaves us in no doubt and events later proved who Jesus was.

Jesus had made an amazing claim: he had said that *he* was the *light of the world* – he was claiming to be God. And yet the Pharisees said:

'Here you are, appearing as your own witness; your testimony is not valid.'

(verse 13)

Jesus' response to this was, *'You judge by human standards'* (verse 15), or, in other words, 'You are judging me without knowing all the facts.' The religious leaders would not believe Jesus' claim to be God – they dismissed him, saying he was demon-possessed, or a liar, or a foreigner, or too ignorant to know what he was talking about, or mad. Down the ages servants of God have often been on the receiving end of such insults. They were calling Jesus these things because they were judging him by their own sinful, limited human standards. Jesus was saying to them, 'You don't know all the facts about me. You are not prepared to open your eyes to the possibility that I may be more than I appear to be. Yes, I am a man, made of flesh and blood like you, but I am also the Christ, the Anointed One sent from the Father. If you were not spiritually blind you would be able to see that I am not a mere man. As it is, you are making hasty judgments about me. Don't just judge from a human point of view. Ask God to open your eyes.'

Amazing claims justified

Jesus said to the Jewish leaders,

'You are from below; I am from above. You are of this world; I am not of this world. I told you that you would die in your sins; if you do not believe that I am the one I claim to be, you will indeed die in your sins.'

(John 8:23–24)

Jesus was making some extravagant claims about who he was. Here he was saying that if they came to him in faith he would forgive them and make them clean from their sins. He was saying, 'I am the only one who can do that for you. If you don't come to me for cleansing from your sins, then you will never be clean in this life or the next.'

After this he said,

'When you have lifted up the Son of Man, then you will know that I am the one I claim to be and that I do nothing on my own but speak just what the Father has taught me.'

(John 8:28)

By *the Son of Man* Jesus meant himself, and by the term *lifted up* he was referring to his own crucifixion. He was saying to them, 'When I am crucified you will really know that the claims I have been making are true – you will know that I am indeed the Messiah.'

And Jesus' prediction indeed came true, because when he was crucified,

From the sixth hour until the ninth hour darkness came over all the land.

And at the moment of Jesus' death

the curtain of the temple was torn in two from top to bottom. The earth shook and the rocks split. The tombs broke open and the bodies of many holy people who had died were raised to life. They came out of the tombs, and after Jesus' resurrection they went into the holy city and appeared to many people.

(Matthew 27:45, 51–53)

All these amazing happenings were evidences that the death of Jesus was no ordinary event: it was the death of the Son of God.

When the centurion and those with him who were guarding Jesus saw the earthquake and all that had happened, they were

terrified, and exclaimed, 'Surely he was the Son of God!'
(Matthew 27:54)

Everyone in the Jerusalem area knew that at the time of Jesus' death something unique and very powerful had happened. The members of the Sanhedrin, seeing the darkness of the sky and the earthquake, must have been petrified. And the Roman centurion who had supervised Jesus' crucifixion was cut to the heart and his spiritual blinkers were removed in an instant; he suddenly knew without doubt that Jesus really was God. We can imagine how terrible he must have felt. He had ordered Jesus to be nailed to the cross, thinking he was just a man, and he then discovered that in fact he was God. The Roman must have been terrified by the knowledge that he had just crucified the Son of God.

'The truth will set you free'

Jesus said to the Jews who had believed that he was the Messiah,

'If you hold to my teaching, you are really my disciples. Then you will know the truth, and the truth will set you free.'
(John 8:31–32)

Jesus has given us two descriptions of what a disciple is. One of them occurs in John 13:35:

All men will know that you are my disciples if you love one another.

The other definition is here in John chapter 8: we are Jesus' disciples if we hold to his teaching. Holding to Jesus' teaching means not only knowing it in our minds but holding it in our being – that is, actually *doing* it, letting it take root in our lives, being obedient to it.

Many of us know our Bibles very well, but we have not really let the teaching of Jesus take root in our lives to the point where we actually obey it. So there is hypocrisy in our lives, because we know what Jesus' teaching is and we can tell people all about it, but we don't really *live* it. This form of hypocrisy is particularly common in those of us who are preachers and teachers: we talk and talk about Jesus and his Good News and the Christian life, but our behaviour does not quite match up to our talk. We do not practise what we preach. Being a disciple of Jesus does not mean knowing all about the Bible and having the whole of Christian theology clearly worked out in our minds; it does not mean being able to quote any part of Scripture from Genesis to Revelation; it does not mean being able to read and understand Scripture in the original languages. Being a disciple of Jesus means knowing, holding to, obeying and living Jesus' teaching.

Jesus tells us that if we hold to his teaching, we will know the truth, and the truth will set us free. The people he was talking to needed to be set free: the Jewish religion had degenerated into a rigid, suffocating set of rules which bound people up in spiritual chains. In the Torah, the Jewish Law, there were 617 rules, and every one of them was a chain wrapped around the people. Jesus was saying to them, 'My Word and my Spirit will come into your life and take root in it, and it will tear up all those chains and you will then be free to be the people God really wants you to be.'

Real Christianity is not a matter of rules and regulations and laws. Actually there are very few laws in the Christian message. There are the Ten Commandments and other aspects of Christian teaching we need to obey, but the essence of the gospel is that the Holy Spirit fills a person's life and shows them how they ought to be living, within the general framework of the Law. To the Jews the Law was everything: it was not only the frame of the picture, but the canvas, the colour, the brush-strokes, the detail, everything. But for the Christian the Law is only the frame within which our lives are to be lived: the actual picture is painted by the Holy Spirit in glorious, unique technicolour. Our lives are not meant to be a painting-by-numbers picture. God does not say, 'There must be red number seven here and here, and blue number five here and here.' Our lives are meant to be beautiful and unique, inspired and designed by the Holy Spirit of God. The truth of Jesus sets us free, and so we are free to paint whatever picture God wants us to paint. We are not all meant to be the same; each Christian's canvas is meant to have a unique picture painted on it. This is all possible because when we become Christians the Holy Spirit comes to live inside us, and he is a creative genius.

However, it frequently happens that the Spirit whom Christians have within them becomes bottled up in old, man-made rules, laws and traditions. We keep the new wine of the Spirit in the old wineskins of Law, and so we live in bondage even though we have the Spirit of freedom within us. God wants to tear up the old wineskins so that his Spirit is free to do what he wills. So much of what we think of as Christianity is in fact no more than the church's traditions and cultural values; these may have been a part of church life for generations, but there is no need for us to be bound by them today.

If people do not know Jesus as Saviour yet, then they are bound not by religious law and rules but by sin. When they become Christians those chains of sin are broken by Jesus and the people enjoy a new freedom in Christ. However, once they have been converted it is possible for them to become wrapped up in bondage once more. They may accept the rules and laws of the church culture around them and lose sight of the wonderful freedom which is meant to be theirs in Christ. Religious legalism can restrict and frustrate the work of the gentle Spirit of freedom whom Jesus has put within us. God wants us to be free from the bondage of law, free to be creative, joyful people.

But before we get intoxicated with this freedom, remember that it can easily become lawlessness. Certainly we do not need to obey the ritual laws of the Old Testament which laid down precise rules about how sacrificial animals should be cut up. Definitely we must not be imprisoned in a legalistic trap which makes us think that we can earn our own salvation by keeping the rules. But Jesus said that he came not to destroy the law but to fulfil it (Matthew 5:17). What did he mean?

Jesus did not mean to restore the ritual sacrifices. He himself was to be the once for all sacrifice which abolished the need for sacrifices. Neither did he come to enslave us: *'the truth will set you free'* he said (John 8:32). No, the law which Jesus came to fulfil was the will of God for our benefit, the Commandments and the other moral guidelines laid down in the Old Testament – the way we need to live so that he is glorified.

As we've just been thinking, the pictures we paint are many and varied and should be free and colourful but the frame (the Law) must not be removed or instead of a satisfying decoration in God's house we shall spill over and become meaningless and purposeless daubs all over the wall.

A King and a Father

'I know you are Abraham's descendants. Yet you are ready to kill me, because you have no room for my word. I am telling you what I have seen in the Father's presence, and you do what you have heard from your father.'

'Abraham is our father,' they replied.

'If you were Abraham's children,' said Jesus, 'then you would do the things Abraham did. As it is, you are determined to kill me, a man who has told you the truth that I heard from God. Abraham did not do such things. You are doing the things your own father does.'

'We are not illegitimate children,' they protested. 'The only Father we have is God himself.'

Jesus said to them, 'If God were your father, you would love me ... You belong to your father, the devil, and you want to carry out your father's desire.'

(John 8:37–42, 44)

Jesus said something here which must have been very offensive to the Jews: he said that the devil, not God, was their father. It was true that technically they were Abraham's descendants, but they were not his children in the true, spiritual sense, and so they were not God's children either. If they had truly been Abraham's children they would have been godly, righteous people, as he was: but instead they were plotting to kill Jesus, God's own Son. In the Greek Jesus actually uses the word which must be translated 'bastard'. This word literally means an illegitimate child. By this Jesus was saying that in the spiritual sense – which is what really mattered – the Jews were children born out of wedlock; they were not true children of God. The Jews were saying, 'We are physically the descendants of Abraham, and we follow in his footsteps; we have the Law and the Scriptures. Surely we are God's children.' But Jesus was saying, 'No, these literal, external things do not make you God's children. You are not his children because you do not have a relationship with him. Your faith is all talk and rules and bondage: there is no spiritual reality in it.'

Today people who are not Christians will sometimes talk in rather vague, generalized terms about everyone being a 'child of God'; indeed, some theologians, who claim to be Christians, are just as vague. It is true that in a sense we are all children of God because we were all created by him. But we can only call him our Father if we have a personal relationship with him through Jesus Christ. The Bible gives the name 'children of God' not to the whole of humanity but to those who have accepted Jesus as their Saviour and so have been adopted into the family of God the Father. When we become Christians we become joint heirs with Jesus: he is the Son of God, and we are also sons or daughters of God. He is our great Elder Brother, and we are his little brothers and sisters, and he and all of us share the same heavenly Father.

So the fact that you are a human being does not necessarily make you a child of God in the true sense. To use an analogy, a friend might leave a baby girl in my house for an evening for my wife and me to look after her. Now, the fact that this baby is a child with the same anatomy as my own daughters does not mean that she is my child: she has a completely different genetic heritage from my daughters. I am not the baby's father. Similarly, not all human beings are children of God, but only those who have a personal relationship with him through Jesus.

Christianity is first of all about having a relationship with God. It is not primarily about being a good, kind person, going to church every Sunday, reading the Bible, doing work for charities and so forth – although, of course, if we really are Christians we will tend to be like that. If we do not know Jesus as our Saviour, then we do not know God as our Father.

If we are Christians, then we need to get excited about the fact that we really are the children of God, that God really is our Father. The beginning of the Lord's Prayer should thrill us: *Our Father in heaven* ... To us God is not just *the* Father of humanity in some vague, impersonal sense: he is *our* father in a very personal way. The God who made the universe, who gave a signal and brought the world into being, who said, *'Let there be light'*, and there was light, who created every single atom of matter in the entire cosmos, who made the galaxies and stars and planets, who created every living thing, who made every human being – this incredibly powerful and wise God, the ruler of the universe, is also our Father if we know him through Jesus his Son. We need to grasp the joy and wonder of that truth. We should turn to him and say, 'Lord God, I am grateful that you are not only the King of the universe, but you are also my loving Father.'

We Christians are called to relate to God in these two ways: he is the King, the Creator of all things – and he is also our Father. In that delightful film, *The King and I*, starring Yul Brynner, the King of Siam's many children related to him in these two ways. When he walked into the room, they would all bow down respectfully, because he was the sovereign lord of their country. Then he would snap his fingers and they would all stand up. (I wish I could get that sort of respect in my home!) Then he would summon them to come to him, one by one, and he would have a short word with each of them, the fatherly love in his heart showing through his royal status. He was their King, but he was also their Daddy.

Our relationship to God is something like that. We should fear him, because he is the King of the universe: we should be flat on our faces, our hearts filled with humility in his presence. But he is also our heavenly Daddy, and he wants a warm, close, loving relationship with us. Sometimes it's not easy to hold these two elements of our relationship to God in balance – sometimes we forget one or the other of them. But both are true and important. Let's be excited about our relationship with God and let's enjoy it, because it is the privilege of every child of God to know him both as the Almighty King and also as the loving Father.

Jesus not only told the Jews that God was not their Father; he also told them that their real father was in fact the devil! Their attitude and behaviour proved this. The devil, said Jesus, '*was a murderer from the beginning*' (verse 44) and the fact that the Jews wanted to kill Jesus showed that they were being motivated by the devil. Jesus was telling them God's truth, but they would not accept it – they preferred lies. This too showed them to be children of the devil, because the devil *'is a liar and the father of lies'* (verse 44). The Jews thought they were right; they were very religious and sincere, and yet they were disastrously wrong in their beliefs and attitudes.

This is a salutary warning for us today. Sometimes we are so sure that we are right that we go marching boldly on, never stopping to ask God whether he approves of what we are doing, never wondering whether or not we are really going in the right direction. We may in fact be seriously wrong in what we believe or in the way we are doing something, and the real motivation behind it is our own sinfulness, egged on and manipulated and exploited by the devil. We think we can see where we are going, but in fact the devil has blinded us. We need to be careful, because Satan, the father of lies, is out to deceive every Christian, and we can fall into that trap of deception so easily.

'I am!'

At the end of this prolonged argument with the Jews Jesus said,

> *'Your father Abraham rejoiced at the thought of seeing my day; he saw it and was glad.' 'You are not yet fifty years old,' the Jews said to him, 'and you have seen Abraham!' 'I tell you the truth,' Jesus answered, 'before Abraham was born, I am!'*
>
> (verses 56–58)

The Jews were so incensed by this that they wanted to stone Jesus but he *hid himself, slipping away from the temple grounds* (verse 59). Jesus was saying that before Abraham had existed, he, Jesus, had existed. *I am* is actually a translation of one of the Hebrew names of God, so Jesus was claiming to be God, who had always existed and so had been in existence before Abraham had been born. Before Abraham had even been conceived in his mother's womb, Jesus was alive, because he is alive *yesterday and today and for ever* (Hebrews 13:8). We Christians can rejoice that we have a Saviour who was there at the beginning of time and will still be there at the end of time. We have a Saviour who knows every jot and tittle of history, who can always be relied upon, who will never die, who will never grow weary, whose power will never fade or fail.

Many of the modern cults flourish for a few decades while their leaders live, but when they die the movements usually peter out within a few years. The same thing has been true of the numerous heresies and cults which have sprouted up over the centuries; they never last for very long. But in the case of Christianity, the reverse happened. As soon as Jesus had died and been raised from the dead, the church began to mushroom at an astonishing rate and did not die after a few years. The church is different from any other religion because its leader is still alive today and will always be alive. The fact that he is alive has huge implications for us in our everyday Christian living. He is always listening to our prayers, speaking to us and working through us; we can always depend upon him because, being God, he can never fail. He died once and he will never die again. Having entrusted our lives to him, we can be certain that he will take care of us for ever and a day.

Chapter 5

God sustains us

He [Jesus] *spat on the ground, made some mud with the saliva, and put it on the man's eyes. 'Go,' he told him, 'wash in the pool of Siloam' (this word means Sent). So the man went and washed, and came home seeing.*

(John 9:6–7)

Siloam and saliva

In John chapter 9 we read that Jesus met a man who had been born blind. It is important that we understand why Jesus healed him in the way he did.

The biblical text tells us that 'Siloam' means 'Sent'. Centuries before Jesus' time, during the reign of the Jewish King Hezekiah, an invading army had approached Jerusalem from the north. Hezekiah had been terrified about this because the city's only water supply was a spring which welled up outside the city walls. This meant that if the city were besieged the water supply would be cut off, and so the defenders would not be able to hold out for very long. To get around this problem Hezekiah undertook one of the most remarkable engineering feats in the ancient world. He ordered his builders to tunnel through 583 yards of solid rock to create an underground conduit running from the spring, under the wall to the interior of the city. The water thus flowed into a pool about thirty feet wide by fifty feet long, and this became known as the Pool of Siloam, since the water in it had been 'Sent' in from outside the city walls. It was also 'Sent' in the sense that the water had been provided by God in a time of desperate need. Thus the pool came to be associated with God's help and provision. The pool became known as the 'Place of Help', and certain rabbis would work there, offering help and advice to whoever wanted it. So it is very appropriate that Jesus helped the blind man at the 'Place of Help', and he may have deliberately used the symbolism of the place to underline the significance of what he was doing.

The Pool of Siloam is a very powerful image of the way in which God sustains us spiritually today. As Christians we are God's soldiers fighting a war in enemy territory, but we can be sure that although an army is besieging us – armed with the weapons of spiritual harassment, family tensions, stress at work, illness, emotional problems – God always keeps us supplied with his living water, the Holy Spirit. We may be embattled, surrounded on every side by hostile forces and circumstances, and yet we still have God's Holy Spirit welling up within us, a never-failing spring of life which quenches our spiritual thirst and frees our souls and which cannot be cut off or destroyed by any external influence. Every Christian has a Pool of Siloam in his or her life, a pool which can never dry up because God himself is constantly renewing it.

But why did Jesus use saliva in the healing of the blind man? To understand this we need to know a little about the significance of saliva in the ancient world. The medical experts of the day believed it to possess unique healing properties. A Roman writer called Pliny wrote an entire chapter about spit in one of his books! He said that saliva was supposed to be able to cure all sorts of sickness, everything from headaches and eye diseases to foot ailments and even leprosy. Often doctors would anoint wounds and sick parts of the body with medicines dissolved in saliva in the belief that this would enhance the effectiveness of the drugs. Now there may or may not have been some truth in all this remarkable lore about saliva, but I believe that Jesus used saliva in this healing as a kind of visual aid to emphasize what he was doing. Of course, it was not the saliva which cured the man but the power of Jesus; the saliva was merely symbolic. So here we can see Jesus taking an ordinary substance, taking the commonplace healing lore of his time, and using it as an agent for a miraculous healing.

That principle is to be found in many places in John's Gospel. For example, take the Feeding of the five thousand in chapter 6. There Jesus was given a few loaves of bread and a few fish and with them he worked a mighty miracle. In the hands of the Master these simple, ordinary things became the substance of a miracle. In the hands of the King humble things become great things because he touches them with his power and uses them for his glory. So in the case of the blind man he took the saliva (there's nothing could be more ordinary than that!) and transformed it into a powerful instrument of God's authority.

There is a vital principle here which all Christians need to understand and make their own. God will gladly take any ordinary, everyday thing which we offer to him, whether it be our time, our money, our possessions, our abilities, and he will touch it with his divine power and transform it so that it will no longer be ordinary but extraordinary. What matters is not how talented we are but how available to God we are, the issue is not *what* you can give to God but *whether* you give it to him. A Christian may be spiritually mature, multi-talented, well educated and intelligent, but all of that ability will be useless unless it is given over to God. Some Christians, on the other hand, seem to be in the grip of feelings of inferiority: they see themselves as unintelligent, spiritually immature and talentless. They feel that there is not much that they can offer God: they think, 'Surely my miserable little contribution to the Lord's work will be next to useless!' However, God is not remotely interested in our own assessment of our gifts, whether that assessment is a high one or a low one. God says to us, 'If you will give your abilities to me I will take them and use them and make something special out of them.' If God can take even some spit and use it to heal someone of blindness, he can certainly take our talents and use them! No matter how mediocre and feeble and pathetic we may think our gifts are, God can transform them and use them powerfully.

Our weakness and inadequacy, if placed in the hands of Jesus, can accomplish far more than the greatest strength and adequacy. Jesus is the source of our power to make a difference in the world, to overcome the evil in the world. Paul wrote,

God chose the foolish things of the world to shame the wise; God chose the weak things of the world to shame the strong.
(1 Corinthians 1:27)

We are called to be indwelt by the Holy Spirit to confound the wise and the powerful, not to take them on at their own game in a clash of power in our own strength. We are called to give all that we have, however little it may be, into God's hands so that he can take it and use it for his glory and for the furthering of his divine purposes in the world.

Who sinned?

In this marvellous healing story in John chapter 9 Jesus encounters a man in desperate need, and is moved with compassion for him. He uses some of his saliva to make some mud, places it on the man's eyes, tells him to go and wash in the Pool of Siloam, and the man's sight is completely restored. This was an amazing miracle, since the man had never been able to see before.

But then the disciples ask an interesting question about the man who had been blind:

'Rabbi, who sinned, this man or his parents, that he was born blind?'

(verse 2)

Since they had been conditioned by the thinking of their Jewish culture, their basic assumption was that the man had been born blind because someone had sinned, either the man himself or one or both of his parents. But Jesus' answer to their question is revolutionary:

'Neither this man nor his parents sinned ... but this happened so that the work of God might be displayed in his life.'

(verse 3)

This is still very much a live issue today. Is sin the cause of sickness? In a *general* sense the answer to that question is yes. When a society or a group of people ignore God's laws, sickness will inevitably result sooner or later. When sin came into the world through the Fall, sickness and disease came in with it. In our society today we can clearly see that a sinful lifestyle results in sickness. The most obvious example of this is in the area of sexual behaviour. There is a direct link between sexual promiscuity and venereal diseases, the most frightening of them being AIDS, of course. We could think of other examples: where a social system is unjust and certain groups of people are deprived of the means to feed themselves properly, they will become vulnerable to all the diseases caused by malnutrition. So in general terms there is a link between a society's sin and sickness amongst its people.

But what about *individual* cases of sickness? Are we justified in making a connection between a person's sin and their sickness? It was the Jewish understanding that when someone sinned God would send a sickness as a punishment, but Jesus was trying to repudiate that view. He denied that the man had been blind either because of his own sin or his parents' sin. He was saying that the man was blind in order that God's power over sickness and disease might be demonstrated, not so that self-righteous people could enjoy pointing the finger at him all his life and telling him he was sick because he was a sinner.

I believe that usually we have no right to think that a person is sick because of their sin. When we pray for sick people we need to be very careful that our attitude and our words are right, lest we end up judging the sick person, adding a weight of condemnation to a person who already has enough to cope with in being ill. Very occasionally it is the case that a person is sick because of their sin, but a mature Christian can normally discern when that is the case after talking with the person in question. Far too often Christians say or think or subtly suggest that a person is sick because of sin. They are prayed for, and the prayer apparently doesn't work, and so people start thinking, 'This person isn't being healed because of the sin in his or her life,' or 'They aren't being healed because they don't have enough faith.' These are very dangerous, damaging attitudes.

When people try to apply general rules to the subject of sickness and healing, they are usually wrong about any given case of sickness. The reason for this is that God treats us as individuals. Every person's case is different. Thus blanket explanations for why people are sick or why prayers for their healing are not working are usually wrong. Jesus treated people as individuals, and so must we.

In his own time Jesus had to break down a lot of misconceptions about this subject, and if he were here in the flesh with us today he would have to do something similar. He healed the blind man in a rather surprising way, using saliva and mud. This probably surprised the disciples. It would certainly surprise us if someone were healed that way today! But Jesus is greater than all our systems and preconceptions about how people are healed. We don't have to get our thinking and praying and methodology exactly right before God will move in healing power. Sometimes I have heard people pray for sick folk using what I thought to be the wrong words, inadequate theology and faulty, naive medical knowledge, and yet the person in question was truly healed nevertheless! God is so great that he can afford to ignore all our preconceptions and do whatever he chooses to do in his sovereign power. The important thing is not to get our theology of healing right but to get right with God and to know him personally and to let him direct his power through us, just as he worked through Jesus to heal the blind man.

A three-stage conversion

The man who had been born blind came to faith in Jesus as his Saviour in three stages. First of all he thought Jesus was merely a good man: he said,

'The man they call Jesus made some mud and put it on my eyes.'

(verse 11)

But later, having thought more about the miracle which Jesus did, he said, *'He is a prophet'* (verse 17). So now he realized that Jesus was more than a man; he was a very special man – a holy man, a man who possessed the power of God to do miracles, a man whose authority was beyond question. And later still, after the man had been expelled by the religious leaders from the temple, Jesus talked with him, and the man came to realize that Jesus was the Christ. He said to Jesus, *'Lord, I believe,'* and worshipped him (verse 38). The word

'Lord' here is the same word as the one used to address God in worship, so the man had no doubt that Jesus was truly God. The man had been expelled from the temple, with all the social stigma which that involved, but he had gained something far better: he had come to know the Lord of the temple.

Acts chapter 14 describes how Paul and Barnabas were in a town called Lystra, and there Paul healed a man who had been lame from birth. The onlookers were so impressed by this that they declared,

'The gods have come down to us in human form!'

(verse 11)

And then they attempted to worship the two men. But Paul and Barnabas tried to stop them, saying,

'Men, why are you doing this? We too are only men, human like you.'

(verse 15)

By contrast, here in John chapter 8 Jesus does not try to prevent the man from worshipping him, because it is right that he should do so: the man knows that Jesus is God, and God ought to be worshipped by human beings.

So the man progressed in his understanding of Jesus from thinking that he was merely a good man, to thinking he was a great prophet, to knowing that he was the Son of God. The same spiritual journey has been repeated in the lives of countless millions of people ever since that time. Today there are many people who think Jesus was just a good man who went around helping people. And there are some people who know that he was more than that; they see him as a great spiritual and moral leader whose teaching and example are still an inspiration to us today. And then there are the people who finally come to the stage of recognizing that Jesus is God, and fall down on their faces and worship him, asking him to come into their lives as their Lord and Saviour and giving their lives over to him. In any given church there will be people at all three of these stages, because they are the stages which we all go through in being converted.

It is not enough to admire Jesus as a good man or as a spiritual leader. We must worship him as our God and surrender ourselves to his lordship. Nothing less will do. We must recognize that the four gospels present to us a Person who is unlike any other man who lived. There is no-one else in all of history to equal Jesus. There is no other book like the New Testament, which tells us about him. In all the annals of human history, there is no-one who even comes close to Jesus in holiness, righteousness, integrity, love, authority, wisdom and miraculous power, simply because he was the only God-man who ever lived. All other people have been merely people. Jesus, as well as being a man, was also God, and his personality exhibited all the character traits of God.

Those who have never acknowledged him as God need to do so if they are to be saved from their sins by him. But now a word of warning to Christians, who were converted some time ago, perhaps many years in the past. They experienced Jesus and gave their lives to him and became saved, but since then their love for him has cooled somewhat. At one time they worshipped him as God, but for a long while they have been relating to him as if he were somehow less than God, as if he were just a great prophet. Really this is backsliding, not backsliding in one's behaviour but in one's concept of who and what Jesus is. When we have been Christians for a long time there is a temptation for us not to take Jesus as seriously as we once did. We become blasé and casual in our relationship with him. His Word no longer has the same cutting edge that it used to have in our lives. If that is our situation, Jesus is saying to us today, 'I was God when you were converted, and I am still God today. I wanted you to worship me then and I still want your worship now. You said then that I was the absolute Lord of your life, but it's no longer true, is it? You no longer respect my divine authority as you once did. I still want to be your absolute Lord today.'

Our attitude to Jesus must always be, 'He is my God, so I must obey him. His Word must be the basis for my whole life. It must shape my thinking patterns, not just once, a long time ago, but continually, here and now and throughout my life I must think about other people in the way that Jesus thinks about them. I must live my life and do my work and conduct all my relationships in the way that pleases Jesus. Everything I do must be an act of worship to him, for he is my God.'

Spiritual blindness

Spiritual blindness is a condition which sets in over a prolonged period of time. With physical blindness, our eyesight may deteriorate gradually, so that we are not immediately aware of it. Then finally we will notice that we don't see things as well as we used to, and so we go to the optician to get some glasses or contact lenses. With spiritual blindness our vision becomes increasingly obscured, and we will be unaware that it is happening.

We can see from what the Pharisees say as they investigate the healing of the blind man that they themselves are spiritually blind. Jesus said,

'For judgment I have come into this world, so that the blind will see and those who see will become blind.'

(verse 39)

Although the Pharisees could see physically, they were blind spiritually: they just could not see that Jesus was the Messiah – they *would* not see it. They had the Law, they worshipped in the temple regularly, but all their religion was useless; they were unable to see who Jesus really was.

Of course, before they are converted people are spiritually blind: but then Jesus takes the veil from their eyes and they can see who he is and they can see the kingdom of God. But even after we have become Christians it is possible to become spiritually blind once again, to varying degrees. We may think we have everything sorted out and we're walking faithfully with God, but all the while we are heading in the wrong direction, unable to see our sin and the wrongness of the direction we are taking.

One of the chief symptoms of spiritual blindness is a refusal to be convinced by the facts and by sound biblical argument. I have encountered this many times. One can try to convince the spiritually blind person about a particular issue, and one can try over and over again, but it never makes any difference: it's like banging your head against a brick wall. They have shut their eyes and ears to what God is saying through his Word; they refuse to face up to the issue, because doing so would be too uncomfortable.

We can clearly see this stubbornness in the Pharisees. They just would not listen to what the man who had been blind had to say. In John 9:15 we read that they asked the man how he had received his sight, and the man gave them a straight answer:

'[Jesus] *put mud on my eyes … and I washed, and now I see.*'

Then they discussed it amongst themselves and then questioned the man again. But they still did not believe him, so they dragged in his parents and interrogated them. Then they summoned the man once more and told him, *'Give glory to God'* (verse 24). This was a Jewish legal phrase which was a command to the person to speak truthfully, similar to our modern witness' oath to tell the truth, the whole truth and nothing but the truth. Witnesses coming before the Sanhedrin would be told the same thing, and it meant that they had to be truthful, since to lie would be to dishonour God. Once again the man who had been blind gave them a straight answer:

'One thing I do know: I was blind but now I see!'

And then once again they asked him what Jesus had done to him. Finally he answered,

'I have told you already and you did not listen. Why do you want to hear it again? Do you want to become his disciples too?'

(verse 27)

Despite the man's honesty and consistent testimony, they would not believe that he had been born blind and that Jesus had healed him. Nothing would ever convince them because they had already decided that they were not going to be convinced.

Spiritual blindness has at its heart a stubborn resistance to the Word of God and an utter refusal to look at the facts honestly. There is a total inability to say, 'In this particular situation I might be wrong, and perhaps I need to think about this more carefully.' We need to be sure that we ourselves do not fall into this trap. It is so tempting to decide that we were right all along, basing our decision on just half the facts, when an objective assessment of all the facts might show that we are actually wrong.

A second characteristic of spiritual blindness which stands out clearly in this passage is a tendency to become angry. In counselling people I have frequently encountered this anger. They have already made up their minds that they are not going to consider anyone else's point of view, and they become increasingly angry as the conversation goes on. We can see this anger in the Pharisees; they ended up hurling insults at the man who had been blind (verse 28). When the man calmly answered them with the irrefutably logical argument that since Jesus was doing such amazing miracles, he must be a man sent from God, they angrily replied,

'You were steeped in sin at birth; how dare you lecture us!'
(verse 34)

In Jewish culture to call someone *steeped in sin at birth* was a terrible insult: it was a crude, rude, vulgar, abusive thing to say. It was a total rejection of the person concerned, viewing him as human rubbish. Clearly, this was not the behaviour of people whose minds and tongues were under God's control. Spiritual blindness often results in a great deal of turmoil and anger festering within people. They are blind in the spiritual sense and stumble about, walking into hard, sharp objects and injuring themselves, blaming everyone else for their pain except themselves.

For their wilful refusal to see the truth the Pharisees came under the judgment of Jesus. He told them,

'If you were blind, you would not be guilty of sin; but now that you claim that you can see, your guilt remains.'
(verse 41)

Because they claimed to be able to see, to know the truth, they were in fact unable to see: their arrogant insistence that they were right made them spiritually blind. They would not admit their sin, and so their blindness remained. The only way to remove spiritual blindness is to go right back to square one, to start again with repentance.

Some of the most important and fruitful times in my own spiritual life have been the times when I was agonizing in my spirit about the rightness or wrongness of an issue or a decision. I had to ask God, 'Lord, if there is anything in my attitude to this matter which is sinful and carnal, I really am sorry about it.' And with that word 'sorry' light begins to dawn: humility begins to lift the burden of spiritual blindness. If we are adamant and arrogant, we will become and remain spiritually blind. If we are humble and repentant we will remain spiritually clear-sighted.

Some of us may experience a massive removal of blindness: in a moment we will suddenly realize how blind we have been through all those years. For some people conversion itself is like that, like seeing the world in a completely different light. But as Christians, through our own sin, we may become progressively spiritually blind. A whole series of veils will obscure our vision. In Jewish weddings the bride would wear a veil, and once the ceremony had been conducted it would be removed and the groom would be able to see her face clearly. In Scripture the idea of a veil is often used as a metaphor for spiritual blindness. As each veil is added, the person becomes less able to see clearly. Eventually there are so many veils that they are completely blinded. Progressively God's revelation is hidden and it becomes increasingly difficult to get back to a condition of spiritual clear-sightedness. In order to cure us of our blindness God has to remove veil after veil, all the layers of blindness which we have brought upon ourselves through our sin, ignorance and defiance of what he has said in the past. Every time God says something to us and we disobey what he has said our vision becomes a little bit more blurred. Because we have not done what he wants this time we are less able to see clearly what he wants us to do the next time. This is why disobedience is such a dangerous thing for Christians. It blurs our vision so that we are unable to see what God is saying, and as a result we will have wrong attitudes, we will make wrong decisions and we will become increasingly distressed emotionally and spiritually. All this is the result of simply not being able to see straight, of no longer being able to see the living Christ in all his power and glory.

The cure for spiritual blindness is very simple, but very humbling: we need to repent, to say sorry, to start again, trusting that God will restore our spiritual eyes to full health.

Chapter 6

The Good Shepherd

I tell you the truth, I am the gate for the sheep ... whoever enters through me will be saved ... I have come that they may have life, and have it to the full.

I am the good shepherd. The good shepherd lays down his life for the sheep ... I know my sheep and my sheep know me—just as the Father knows me and I know the Father—and I lay down my life for the sheep.

(John 10:7, 9, 10, 14–15)

Here in John chapter 10 we have one of the best-known passages in the Bible, where Jesus calls himself *the good shepherd.* In this passage Jesus twice uses the phrase, *'I tell you the truth'* (verses 1 and 7). This expression occurs many times in John's Gospel, and its function is to tell us that what Jesus is saying here is of the very greatest importance. The fact that Jesus is our Shepherd is a very precious truth.

In order fully to understand the passage we need to know a little about the way in which shepherds worked in the ancient Near East. In the centre of Israel there is an upland plateau on which many shepherds used to keep their flocks. It was fairly fertile land, so there was plenty of grass for the sheep to eat, but it was a remote, wild place bisected by deep ravines. So the shepherds had to keep a careful watch on the sheep to ensure that they did not fall off cliffs or wander into the ravines and get lost. Losing just one sheep meant a major loss of income for a poor shepherd. In the ancient Near East sheep were kept mainly for their wool rather than their meat, and so there would have been a relationship between the shepherd and his animals: they would have been his friends, almost his pets.

While modern European shepherds tend to drive and control their sheep with dogs, the Middle Eastern shepherd used to tend the sheep alone, and instead of driving them in front of him he would lead them, making sure that the way ahead was safe, free from wild animals or dangerous crevasses. The sheep would follow behind in safety. One of the things which the picture of Jesus as the Good Shepherd shows us is that he has gone on ahead of us, the sheep, to make the way safe for us. Jesus doesn't look after us in the way the European shepherd looks after his sheep; he doesn't send his watchdogs to harass and chivvy us along. The Good Shepherd goes ahead and faces all the danger for us. He has gone ahead into the ultimate dangerous ravine, the valley of death itself, by sacrificing his own life for us on the cross. He has gone into the valley and passed through it, emerging victorious on the other side into God's glorious presence. Because Jesus has done this for us we too can pass safely through death into God's eternal life.

Called by name

Jesus said that the shepherd of the sheep *calls his own sheep by name and leads them out* (John 10:3). There is a story from the ancient world which helps us to understand this. Once a traveller was passing over the plateau in central Israel, and one night he came to a cave where a number of shepherds were gathered around a fire for warmth. He stayed with them overnight. In the morning he noticed that the flocks of all the shepherds were intermingled. There were no obvious markings on the animals, so he wondered how the shepherds were ever going to work out which sheep belonged to whom. But one by one the shepherds walked to the edge of the mixed flock and called out the names of their sheep. Each of the sheep was unique and each had been given a name by its shepherd. And as their names were called out, the sheep went to the shepherd until all his flock was gathered round him. Each of those sheep was important to the shepherd: each was known by him, and they all knew him.

Jesus the Good Shepherd is concerned about us, his sheep: we are all precious and important to him. When we consider that we are just solitary individuals, members of a human race about five thousand million strong, living on one of the smallest planets in our solar system which is just one of about one hundred thousand million stellar systems in our Milky Way galaxy, which is just one of billions of galaxies in the universe, it seems unlikely that God should be concerned about me or you. But that is the truth: the Good Shepherd cares about us, and if we are Christians we are members of his flock and he knows us by name. When Jesus rose from the dead and came to Mary in the Garden of Gethsemane she at first thought he was the gardener. But then he called her by name, and she suddenly recognized him (see John chapter 20). And today Jesus knows his sheep by name and cares deeply about us as individuals, because, like the shepherd of the ancient world, he cares about every single sheep of his flock.

Listen to the Good Shepherd's voice

Jesus said his sheep

'will never follow a stranger; in fact, they will run away from him because they do not recognise a stranger's voice.'

(John 10:5)

When a shepherd called his sheep by name, other sheep would hear his voice, but, not recognizing it as their own shepherd's voice, would not go to him. Similarly, the Good Shepherd's sheep know the sound of his voice and will not follow any other voice. If we are Christians we have been given an ability to hear Jesus' voice. If only we will listen carefully, we will be able to tell when we are hearing some other voice, which will lead us away from the right path and into some dangerous ravine. Many Christians don't listen carefully enough: they hear all sorts of different voices and think they need to obey them all. But the voice of Jesus is the only voice we need to obey, and we have been given the ability to hear it clearly for our own protection.

As I have matured as a Christian I have found that I have become increasingly aware of how sinful I really am, and consequently how big and powerful God's forgiveness is. I have also found that I have become more and more aware of what is right and wrong. I don't always *do* what is right, but I more often *know* what is right. I am not talking about obvious decisions such as 'Should I steal this money or not?' The Ten Commandments lay down some basic guidelines for our behaviour. But in life there are a great many judgments and decisions which we have to make, and the rightness or wrongness of any course of action is often far from obvious. But increasingly I find that I instinctively know what is right in such a situation: I cannot precisely say why it is right, but I feel sure that it is. This is because I have become better at hearing the voice of Jesus telling me what is right, and I am better able to distinguish between his voice in any situation and the other voices which talk to me, the voices of people or even of the devil. Often those voices are subtly disguised, but I am able to see through that.

When people first become Christians, they are mere lambs in the Good Shepherd's flock. They have not had time to build up their relationship with him, and they are not very good at hearing his voice. So he has to take special care of them to make sure that they do not respond to deceptive voices which will lead them into trouble and injury. Often what the other voices say will be appealing: they will lure us into sin, making it appear attractive and inviting. Or else they will tempt us into some activity which is not sinful in itself, but is not what Jesus wants us to be doing at that particular time. Many of us have found that taking such a wrong turning, while it appeared to be pleasant, in the end turned out to be painful and disastrous. The result was a period spent wandering in a spiritual wilderness. But we can avoid such damaging experiences if we will only listen to the Shepherd's voice and reject what the other voices say.

Food for the sheep

The Good Shepherd's sheep will *come in and go out, and find pasture* (John 10:9). In other words, the Shepherd provides food for his sheep. As I mentioned earlier, the Middle Eastern shepherds generally kept their sheep only for wool and didn't slaughter them for their meat, so there was a long-term relationship between the shepherd and his sheep. He didn't lead them to pasture in order to make them fat for slaughter; he fed them simply to provide for their needs. Our Good Shepherd feeds us not for his own gain but because he cares about us.

I am not just talking about food for our bodies; God does indeed provide that for us, along with everything else we need. I am talking about spiritual food: the food which our spirits need to be healthy, strong and growing. Sadly, some Christians are starving to death spiritually. They have all the physical food they need, but they almost totally ignore their need for spiritual food. God provides this food for us in a variety of ways:

through worship, prayer, fellowship and, most of all, through his Word, the Bible. He has provided all the food we need: it is up to us to take advantage of that provision. The Good Shepherd leads us to the rich pastures, but only we can actually eat the food there: he can't make us eat it.

Good and bad leaders

'I am the good shepherd. The good shepherd lays down his life for the sheep. The hired hand is not the shepherd who owns the sheep. So when he sees the wolf coming, he abandons the sheep and runs away. Then the wolf attacks the flock and scatters it. The man runs away because he is a hired hand and cares nothing for the sheep.'

(John 10:11–13)

When Jesus spoke about the Good Shepherd who lays down his life for the sheep, he was speaking about his own coming crucifixion. Then he went on to talk about hired shepherds who looked after the sheep but did not own them. By this Jesus meant the leaders of God's people. Jesus is the great Shepherd of the flock, while church leaders are under-shepherds working for him. In using this analogy he was following the pattern of the Old Testament, in which the leaders of Israel were often described as shepherds of God's flock.

All of us who are in church leadership today need to ask ourselves whether we are truly concerned about the flock and whether we give ourselves to them and for them sacrificially. Or are we the kind of leaders who are happy to be in leadership when things are going well, but when the wolves come – that is, problems, tensions, persecution, conflict – we run off because it has all become too costly and because we don't really care about the flock? We may not literally run away, but we may do so spiritually; we may back away from real commitment to the people in our church. Are we the sort of leaders who put the flock first or do we instead put our own comfort, happiness and status first? Do we lay down our lives for the sheep or is looking after our own skin our first priority? If we are really concerned about the flock, we will gladly take no end of abuse, criticism, misunderstanding and pressure on their account. All leaders need to model their leadership on the example of Jesus, who literally gave his life for the sheep of his flock. He went through the ravine of death in order to lead his sheep to safety, to eternal life. He said,

'Greater love has no-one than this, that he lay down his life for his friends.'

(John 15:13)

Only one flock

Jesus said,

'I have other sheep that are not of this sheep pen. I must bring them also. They too will listen to my voice, and there shall be one flock and one shepherd.'

(John 10:16)

Jesus was talking to an audience of Jews, and by the *other sheep* he meant the Gentiles. His flock was to include not only Jews but Gentiles also. Jesus was not content for his flock to remain the same size: it was his intention that it should grow enormously, extending beyond the Jewish nation to all the nations of the world.

We still need to hear that message today. The good news about Jesus is not just for our own race but for all people everywhere. The gospel is not just for the people who are already Christians but also for those who have not yet received Jesus as their Saviour. The world needs to hear that the Good Shepherd is alive today, that he cares for people, that his gospel is real and powerful and can change lives. You don't need to be a philosopher or a sociologist to see that our society today is disintegrating all around us: we desperately need to hear the good news about Jesus. Family life is collapsing; millions of children and teenagers are growing up without any moral teaching; violent crime is becoming ever more commonplace; vast numbers of people are becoming drawn into occult bondage; the well-off are becoming richer and more selfish while the poor are becoming poorer and more desperate. Our society is under impossible stress and is rapidly falling apart.

There is only one answer to the appalling mess we are in, and that is that people should turn to Jesus Christ as their Lord and Saviour. We Christians need to be aware of the enormous pressures and stresses which are at work in our country; and we need to discover for ourselves that the answer is Jesus and the new quality of life which he offers, and then to pass that answer on to other people.

Some of us may live in parts of the country, inner city areas, for example, where the fracture lines in our society are very evident. Others may live in more sheltered districts, the countryside or the suburbs, but even there the forces of disintegration are at work. Wherever we live we are surrounded by people of all ages and all types who are lost sheep, wandering about in despair, falling down dangerous ravines and injuring themselves or even dying. Their lostness and pain may be concealed to some extent, indeed, they may even hide it from themselves, locking it away deep inside their hearts, but it is real none the less. Today the Good Shepherd wants us to bring new sheep into his flock so that he can protect them and provide for them.

Jesus said, *'there shall be one flock and one shepherd'* (verse 16). He intended his church to be one united people. What a mess we have made of his original plan! Throughout the history of the church there have been schisms, the flock being divided into many fragments. Today there are a great many different Christian denominations, often antagonistic towards one another. But the truth is that God did not specifically design our denominational labels: he doesn't make us Baptists, Anglicans, Methodists, Pentecostals, Brethren, Salvationists, charismatics, Catholics, Orthodox or whatever. The really vital distinction between people is whether or not they have received Jesus as their Lord and Saviour. Jesus divided humanity into the sheep (those who know Jesus) and the goats (those who don't know him, Matthew 25:31–46). What God is concerned to establish is whether we know Jesus.

Neither has God commanded all the different denominations to get together into some kind of interdominational super-church with a unified structure. I am convinced that as well as trying to organize agreement with other churches which may only paper over the cracks of our differences, God wants all of the churches to get on together with the task of evangelism. We need to increase the total size of Jesus' flock, rather than trying to weld all the churches into one church without actually adding any new people to it. We may belong to different church groupings, but we all know and love and serve the same Lord Jesus Christ; he is our unity.

In my travels abroad I have met a great many Christians from all sorts of backgrounds. Many of them could not speak English, so we could not communicate very well, but it was very evident to me that these people were true Christians. Some of them came from church backgrounds very different from my own. In my view their theology was wrong in certain respects, they attached unnecessary importance to external things like dress and ritual, their understanding of Scripture was defective, and so on. Yet these people obviously knew and loved Jesus. My response had to be, 'Lord, if you love these people, then I've got to love them too. I praise you for what you are doing in their lives.' Denominationally they were a million miles away from my Baptist roots, but we were united by our common love for Jesus.

I am a convinced Baptist. I think believer's baptism by full immersion is important and significant, and I strongly believe in the priesthood of all believers. But I am a Christian first and a Baptist second: I am in unity with all people everywhere who truly know and love Jesus Christ. Unity in the Holy Spirit is a unity which transcends every denominational barrier. It is sadly the case that there will be some Baptists who will not get into heaven, because the only way into heaven, into the presence of the Father, is through a relationship with the Son, Jesus. There are some Baptist churchgoers who think that being a Baptist will save them: but only Jesus can save them. And the same is true of all other denominations. We will not get into heaven by wearing a badge saying 'Baptist' or 'Anglican' or 'Methodist'; we will be received into heaven only if we have known and loved the Lord Jesus and have given him our lives.

In the hands of Jesus

'My sheep listen to my voice; I know them, and they know me. I give them eternal life, and they shall never perish; no-one can snatch them out of my hand. My Father, who has given them to me, is greater than all; no-one can snatch them out of my Father's hand. I and the Father are one.'

(John 10:27–30)

In these words Jesus gives us a wonderful assurance about our eternal life in him. If we have given ourselves to him and have accepted him as our Saviour, we are in his hands and no-one can snatch us out of them. More than that, we are doubly secure, because not only are we in Jesus' hands, but in some remarkable way Jesus himself is in the Father's hands. There is nothing in all the universe which can take away from us the salvation and blessings which God has given us in Jesus. We will never wake up one morning and find that our salvation has somehow evaporated overnight; we are loved by God so much that we are locked into Jesus with total security. Nothing and no-one can pluck us out of Jesus' hands, neither the devil nor any power in the world. As the apostle Paul wrote,

I am convinced that neither death nor life, neither angels nor demons, neither the present nor the future, nor any powers, neither height nor depth, nor anything else in all creation, will be able to separate us from the love of God that is in Christ Jesus our Lord.

(Romans 8:38–39)

Rededication

In John 10:22 we read that Jesus was in Jerusalem at the time of the Feast of Dedication. I believe that this Jewish celebration has something very important to say to us today. The Feast of Dedication or Hanukkah was a commemoration of an event which occurred about two centuries before Jesus' lifetime. At that time Israel had been under the rule of a Graeco-Syrian ruler named Antiochus Epiphanes. He was very hostile to the Jews and wished to eradicate the worship of their God Yahweh, instead imposing Greek culture and religion on them. (All this is recorded in the apocryphal books called 1 Maccabees and 2 Maccabees.) The temple in Jerusalem was desecrated, the temple courtyards were turned into brothels, and pig-meat was offered on the altar (this would have been deeply offensive to the Jews, since to them pork was a ceremonially unclean meat). Women who had their children circumcised in the Jewish fashion were crucified with their children hung around their necks. In short, it was a bloody and blasphemous reign of terror.

It is no surprise that the Jews finally rebelled against Antiochus, led by a warrior named Judas Maccabaeus, who broke the power of the despot. The temple was reconsecrated to God and the altar, which had been defiled with pig-meat, was ceremonially cleansed, and pure offerings to God were once more made on the altar. So Hanukkah, the Feast of Dedication, was the time when the Jews celebrated the cleansing and rededication of the temple after the defilement of Antiochus's reign.

Hanukkah is a powerful symbol for us today. It says to us that whatever has happened in our past, however horrendous and loathsome our sins may have been, we can be rededicated to God. He is willing to let us start with him afresh, with a completely clean slate. Many people struggle with oppressive feelings of guilt. They think, 'But I did such awful things in the past! How can God forgive all the sinful things I have said and thought and done?' The truth is that God can take all of our moral dirt and sin and wash it away: we can all have a Hanukkah, a new start through Jesus Christ. The temple in Jerusalem, although it had been defiled, was cleansed and rededicated to God. The Bible says that we are temples of the Holy Spirit (1 Corinthians 6:19); if we have been defiled by our sins, we can be made clean again by Jesus.

Chapter 7

Death: the Final Frontier

Now a man named Lazarus was sick ... [Jesus] *went on to tell them, 'Our friend Lazarus has fallen asleep; but I am going there to wake him up' ... Jesus had been speaking of his death ...*

(John 11:1, 11, 13)

Jesus the conqueror of death

If John chapter 10 was the heart of the gospel in terms of teaching, chapter 11 is the heart of the gospel in terms of action. In chapter 10 Jesus described himself as the Good Shepherd, and displayed his love, gentleness and care for his sheep. In chapter 11 we see Jesus in action as he conquers the greatest enemy of mankind: death itself.

The hugely popular TV science fiction series *Star Trek* begins with the now famous words, 'Space: the final frontier'. Many of us have greatly enjoyed *Star Trek* over the years. However, the real 'Final Frontier' is not space but death, and it was Jesus who 'boldly went' and vanquished it.

For our generation, as for every other in history, death is the ultimate mystery. It has been said that death is the one certain thing about life: whoever we are, we will all die one day. One of the most important things in life is coming to terms with the fact of death. And we can only really come to terms with it through what Jesus has done for us. He has shown us that he himself is the way through death into eternal life. Here in John chapter 11 he not only tells us, *'I am the resurrection and the life'* but proves it to us by raising his friend Lazarus from the dead.

Crossing the Final Frontier

John chapter 11 is in the middle of the gospel, and from this point onwards we see that Jesus' ministry is drawn away from the Sea of Galilee, where the earlier part of his work was concentrated, and closer and closer to Jerusalem, where it would have its final expression and fulfilment in his crucifixion and resurrection. In this final phase of his ministry he often made the two-mile journey from Bethany, where his friends Lazarus, Mary and Martha lived, to Jerusalem. In chapter 12 we read of his triumphal entry into the capital riding on a donkey, but for now he is biding his time, waiting for the right moment.

When Jesus heard that Lazarus was sick, he said,

> *'This sickness will not end in death. No, it is for God's glory so that God's Son may be glorified through it.'*
>
> (verse 4)

So the disciples probably thought Jesus would go and heal Lazarus. But no:

> *When he heard that Lazarus was sick, he stayed where he was two more days.*
>
> (verse 6)

During that time Lazarus died, and only then did Jesus go to Bethany. Now

> *he told them plainly, 'Lazarus is dead, and for your sake I am glad I was not there, so that you may believe. But let us go to him.'*
>
> (verses 14–15)

It seemed to the disciples that Jesus had contradicted

himself. He had said that the sickness would not end in death, which of course they had taken to mean that Lazarus was not going to die; and yet now he was saying that he was already dead. They were probably thinking that Jesus had made a mistake. It did not occur to them that he was going to raise Lazarus from the dead: such a miracle was beyond their imagination at that point. To them, death was indeed the Final Frontier. There was nothing beyond it. As far as they were concerned, nothing and no-one could defeat death. They did not understand that because Jesus was God he could break through even the barrier of death.

The disciples were thinking, 'Jesus is wonderful! We've seen him do amazing miracles! We've seen him go up to people who were totally blind, touch them and give them sight immediately. We've seen Jesus lay his hands on people who were horribly crippled, and they were able to get up and walk. We've seen Jesus touch people who were covered with leprous sores, and their skin was immediately made clean and healthy. All that was wonderful, *but Lazarus is dead!* What can Jesus possibly do for him now? If he had got to him before he died he could have healed him, but it's too late now. No-one can bring someone back from the dead.' And Jesus was thinking, 'You just don't understand yet, do you? You think death is stronger even than I am. But I am stronger than death, because I am God.'

The final word is always God's

Jesus had allowed Lazarus to die so that through his death and resurrection the disciples could enter a whole new dimension of faith. Jesus was using Lazarus's death as a visual aid to show the disciples that nothing was impossible for him, because he was God. He wanted to show them that death was not the Final Frontier, the final word: rather, the final word was his and God's. He would command Lazarus to rise from the dead, and it would indeed happen. Despite all the miracles they had seen him do, the disciples still did not really understand that Jesus was God and that he had the power to do anything. As Jesus says in the book of Revelation, he is *the Alpha and the Omega ... the First and the Last* (Revelation 1:8, 17). He is the *First* because he was with God in the beginning of the universe, and he is the *Last* because he will still be with God at the end of the universe: and because he is the Last he has the last word. Death is not absolute or final: only Jesus is the absolute, the final arbiter.

The disciples needed to learn this vital principle, and we Christians today need to grasp it too. It is this principle which divides immature Christians from those who are going on to maturity in Christ. The mature Christian is learning that the final word is always God's. He or she knows that appearances can be deceptive: things may appear to be going badly for us personally or for our church or for the work for God in which we are involved, but the end result is not in the hands of the devil or of our human adversaries; it is in the hands of God. Men and women of true faith and vision are the ones who know in their hearts that there is no frontier beyond which God cannot go: something may seem impossible to us, but all things are possible with God. There are times when we need to disregard what our physical eyes are telling us and instead see things through our spiritual eyes, through our faith in the Living God who always has the last word.

Once again in this passage we see how the disciples frequently misunderstood what Jesus was talking about. He said,

'Our friend Lazarus has fallen asleep; but I am going to wake him up.'

(verse 11)

Of course, Jesus was using the idea of sleep metaphorically; he knew that Lazarus had indeed died, but since he was going to be raised from death, his dying was like falling asleep, and his resurrection would be like waking up. However, *his disciples thought he meant natural sleep* (verse 13), and everyone knows that if you are sick, plenty of sleep will aid your recovery, so they said, *'Lord, if he sleeps, he will get better'* (verse 12). Here, as so often elsewhere in the gospels, Jesus said something at one level, but the disciples were thinking at a lower level and so misunderstood him.

The humanity of Jesus

In John 11:33–36 we have a wonderfully revealing glimpse of the humanity of Jesus. He and the disciples had reached a place just outside Bethany and he had already spoken with Martha. She then went into the village and told Mary that Jesus wanted to see her. So she ran to him.

When Mary reached the place where Jesus was and saw him, she fell at his feet and said, 'Lord, if you had been here, my brother would not have died.'

When Jesus saw her weeping, and the Jews who had come along with her also weeping, he was deeply moved in spirit and troubled. 'Where have you laid him?' he asked.

'Come and see Lord,' they replied.

Jesus wept.

Then the Jews said, 'See how he loved him!'

(John 11:33–36)

The Greek phrase which the NIV renders as *deeply moved in spirit and troubled* is a little difficult to translate. In classical Greek it was often used to mean the snorting of a horse, but John used it in this context to mean an involuntary noise in the throat. Really it means a sob, gasp, sigh or groan provoked by deep emotional pain. Jesus was so upset by the grief of Mary and her friends that he groaned.

Verse 35 is in fact the shortest verse in the whole Bible: *Jesus wept.* It is appropriate that it should be a verse all by itself, because it is so moving and significant. Jesus had groaned with sadness, and now he wept because his friend Lazarus had died, and he wept for grief-stricken Martha and Mary, who now had no man to provide for them. Jesus was the great God, and yet he was also a real human being, capable of real human emotions. Bereavement is a painful experience, and Jesus felt that pain as much as anyone else does. Because he was really human he understands the trials and sorrows which we all experience. Sometimes when I feel under pressure or hurt or fed up, I am so grateful that Jesus understands how I feel, because he himself has experienced those selfsame feelings. Too often Christians have thought of Jesus as a kind of stained-glass window figure with a halo around his head who looks down piously on the world as if he were only God and not a real man, as if he took on human form without really becoming a man. But Jesus really was human, and so he understands the issues and problems we have to grapple with in our daily lives.

Now I don't completely understand how Jesus could have been both fully God and fully man at the same time (no-one ever has), but I do know that the Bible clearly teaches us that this was indeed the case. The Bible shows us that, without sin, he experienced the full gamut of human emotions, from sadness to joy. Some Christians say that Jesus didn't laugh often, since the Bible doesn't say anything about him laughing. I believe that Jesus laughed so much all the time that the gospel writers took it for granted and so didn't bother to put it in their accounts! There is certainly plenty of evidence in the gospels that Jesus had a wry sense of humour. We also see cases where he was glad about things, and others where he redirected the disciples' joy so that it was not merely joy about a superficial thing but joy about something really important.

The resurrection and the life

Jesus said something utterly amazing to Martha:

'I am the resurrection and the life. He who believes in me will live, even though he dies: and whoever lives and believes in me will never die. Do you believe this?'

(verses 25–26)

She didn't really understand what he was saying, but she replied,

'Yes, Lord ... I believe that you are the Christ, the Son of God, who was to come into the world.'

(verse 27)

We first of all need to understand that when Jesus said *'whoever lives and believes in me will never die'*, he was not saying that his followers would not physically die. Even the apostles died physically, indeed, some of them were brutally executed. Jesus was not talking about physical life but eternal life. All those who believe in Jesus will have eternal life, even though their physical bodies will die and decay. That eternal life starts the moment someone believes in Jesus, and after their physical death it will continue, as they live in the presence of Jesus for ever.

This is why the Christian message is so important. We Christians are the living among the dead, and we must tell them that by believing in Jesus they too can have life, life which will transform their existence here and now and which will continue in a wonderful way after the death of their bodies. We need to tell people that death is no longer the Final Frontier, because Jesus has gone beyond it and has opened up the way for all of us to go with him into eternal life. If we believe in Jesus, death no longer need be a terrible, hateful thing: it is merely the gateway to a greater, closer experience of the Jesus whom we have come to know and love here and now.

In previous generations sex used to be the thing which people did not mention in polite conversation; today death is the great taboo subject. Many people today are terrified of death; they can't bear to think about it or even to hear the subject mentioned. They try to live as if they will never die, as if death does not exist. But because Jesus has died and risen from the dead in our place, we need no longer fear death if we put our faith in him as our Saviour. We Christians need to tell people today that they can be free from the fear of death. Jesus has robbed death of its power over us. As Paul wrote:

'Death has been swallowed up in victory.'

> *'Where, O death is your victory?*
> *Where, O death, is your sting?'*

... thanks be to God! He gives us the victory through our Lord Jesus Christ.

(1 Corinthians 15:54–57)

This means that every person on the face of the earth can have eternal life, if they will put their trust in Jesus. The sad thing is that the offer of eternal life is so simple that many people can't believe it and accept it; they think there must be more to it than that. But the truth is that the moment we believe in Jesus we step from the land of the dying into the land of the living.

The divinity of Jesus

While this passage vividly shows us the humanity of Jesus, it also clearly shows us his divinity, for no-one but God could have raised Lazarus from the dead. Here in the very same passage we see both of Jesus' natures, the divine and the human. In verse 27 we read of Mary affirming her belief in his divinity:

'Yes, Lord … I believe that you are the Christ, the Son of God, who was to come into the world.'

And then in verses 38–44 we see Jesus acting with the authority of God as he gives new life to his dead friend.

This passage also contains one of those little details which demonstrate clearly that all of this really happened and was recorded by an eye-witness. Jesus told them to remove the stone from the tomb, but Martha protested that now, after four days in a hot climate, Lazarus's body would have decomposed to such a degree that there would be a foul odour inside the tomb. To include personal details like that was an unusual or even unprecedented thing to do in the literature of the time. If John had been making all this up, he simply would not have written his gospel in that way.

We can imagine that Martha's comment made Jesus smile just a little bit, even in such a sad situation, because she, along with all the others, did not understand what he was going to do. They probably thought he merely wanted to see Lazarus's body so that he could pay his last respects to him. They had no idea that Jesus was about to do a mighty miracle. He gently rebuked Martha for what she had said:

'Did I not tell you that if you believed, you would see the glory of God?'

(verse 40)

Then they took away the stone, Jesus briefly prayed to his Father and then he

called in a loud voice, 'Lazarus, come out!' The dead man came out, his hands and feet wrapped with strips of linen, and a cloth around his face.

(verses 43–44)

Although Jesus said this in a loud voice and with

authority, I believe he also said it gently and not stridently, because it was his dear friend he was calling out from the tomb. The cave in which Lazarus had been entombed was probably part of a cemetery, so there would have been many other tombs nearby. I believe that if Jesus had simply said, 'Come out!' there would have been a mass resurrection! Jesus was God, and he possessed the power of God, so he could have raised all the dead to life. But he used Lazarus's name and so focused his power on one individual.

Jesus had talked to his followers about eternal life and resurrection, and now he had given them a totally convincing demonstration of his power as the Son of God to defeat death.

Therefore many of the Jews who had come to visit Mary, and had seen what Jesus did, put their faith in him.

(verse 45)

No wonder! This miracle must have created a huge sensation in the local district – people would have been talking about it for many days afterwards. What could be more amazing than a man dying and then being brought back to life after four days?

And this biblical story is not just that; it also has relevance to us today, at the close of the twentieth century. The power of Jesus which raised Lazarus back to life is still available to us today if we will trust Jesus and ask him for it. Jesus has power over spiritual death, because on the cross and in his resurrection he defeated death so that we could share in that victory and have eternal life. Moreover, Jesus has power over physical death. He has broken through the Final Frontier, both spiritually and physically.

Here we see a pattern which occurs throughout the gospels: Jesus performs a miracle and many of the people who witness it are convinced by it that he is the Son of God. Jesus still often works in the same way today. People will often not be convinced by words alone; they need a demonstration of the power of Jesus before they will believe in him.

Chapter 8

No pain, no gain

Therefore many of the Jews who had come to visit Mary, and had seen [Jesus raise Lazarus from the dead] *put their faith in him. But some of them went to the Pharisees and told them what Jesus had done. Then the chief priests and the Pharisees called a meeting of the Sanhedrin.*

(John 11:45–47)

Vested interests

The Sanhedrin was the ruling council of the Jewish people. It was composed of two antagonistic factions: the Pharisees and the Sadducees. The Pharisees were very religious, legalistic people who were fiercely committed to obeying every jot and tittle of the 617 Old Testament laws. The Sadducees formed a powerful social class whose chief concern was to protect and maintain their wealth and status. These two groups had different beliefs about the Jewish faith. The Pharisees were rigidly orthodox, while the Sadducees did not believe in the resurrection (that was why they were *sad, you see,* as the old joke goes!). The two groups could never agree among themselves, let alone lead the Jewish people effectively. Both were really interested in the truth, but the truth only as they saw it, not in being truly open to God. They both represented vested interests; the Pharisees the interests of the religious establishment, the Sadducees the interests of the wealthy. With respect to Jesus, the only question the Pharisees were asking themselves was, 'Does what Jesus is doing agree with our understanding of the Law?' The only question the Sadducees were asking was, 'Will what Jesus is doing help to preserve our wealth and our privileged position in society under Roman rule?' None of them were asking, 'Is what Jesus is doing *right?'* Their attitude was,

> *'What are we accomplishing? ... Here is this man performing many miraculous signs. If we let him go on like this, everyone will believe in him, and then the Romans will come and take away both our place* [or temple] *and our nation.'*
>
> (verses 47–48)

They were terrified by what Jesus was doing. They never stopped to consider the fact that Jesus' miracles showed that he was from God and that therefore they should listen to what he was saying. They were so committed to their own view of the truth that they were unable to recognize the genuine article when they saw it. In addition they feared that if the masses followed Jesus a rebellion against Rome would result, and their own privilege and power would be swept away by the Romans as they suppressed the revolt. And so they came to the conclusion that they had to do something about Jesus before it was too late:

> *So from that day on they plotted to take his life.*
>
> (verse 53)

Dodging the Word

Often we Christians today are tempted to commit the same sin as the Pharisees and Sadducees – that is, to take the Word of God, or what God is saying or doing at the present, and to try to twist it so that it fits in with our preconceptions and vested interests. If Jesus says something to us that we don't like because it will be painful and costly to obey, then we try to accommodate it, to move its influence away from ourselves and on to someone else. We try to absorb the weight of what he is saying so that it won't have any real impact on our lives.

It is very easy to sit and hear a sermon preached against a sin which we ourselves are not tempted to commit. For example, we may hear a sermon about the damage caused by gossipping, and since gossip is not one of our besetting sins, we sit there feeling safe and righteous. We enjoy sermons like that because they are rebuking people other than ourselves. We sit there thinking, 'Thank you, Lord, that by your grace I hardly ever gossip. I really pray that this sermon will convict *him* and *her* and *him* ...' We feel pleased with ourselves because we know we are not resisting God's Word.

However, it's a different matter when we hear a sermon or read a Bible passage which convicts us about a sin that we often commit. The Word comes searchingly into our hearts and God is speaking to us directly, but what we sometimes do then is to try to deflect it so that we won't feel its weight; we try to push it towards other people. 'Yes, well, I do commit that sin sometimes ... but *they* commit it much more often, so they are the people who should take notice of this sermon. I'm free to stop listening.' We think about something else until God has given up speaking to us about that particular issue for the time being. Or it may be that we do not recognize the correction God is trying to bring about because we are blinded by the certainty that we are right and cannot see that we are wrong. Why do we try to avoid the impact of God's Word in our lives? Because obeying God is often costly.

Facing up to what Jesus had done in raising Lazarus from the dead would have been costly for the members of the Sanhedrin. For the Sadducees, it would have meant having to abandon their disbelief in the resurrection; no-one likes to have to give up a pet belief or unbelief. For the Pharisees it would have meant recognizing that the way to eternal life was not through scrupulously observing every last detail of the Law but through faith in Jesus as the Messiah: that would have called for a total reorientation of their lives. But, of course, the Sanhedrin members did not want their safe, secure, comfortable lives to be revolutionized by Jesus, and so they sidestepped the significance of Lazarus's resurrection: they simply refused to consider it seriously.

The point of pain

If something causes us pain, that is usually a sure indication that that is an area of need in our lives. If part of the biblical message distresses us, that is where God wants to touch us and heal us. When I lie down on the dentist's chair and he probes around in my mouth, speaking bits of secret dentists' code to his assistant, I don't mind too much if it doesn't hurt. But if he finds somewhere in my mouth where it hurts, that is sure to be the place where he needs to do some work. He says the dreaded word 'cavity', and I know I'm in for a highly unpleasant drilling session, either then or a few days later. It would be foolish of me to protest, 'Look, feel free to poke all the other teeth, but leave that one alone, because it hurts! We'll dispense with the drilling and the fillings, thanks very much!' But he would say, 'Of course that tooth hurts: it's got decay in it. If I don't deal with it, the pain will get much worse!' So the pain is an indication that the tooth needs some attention. Similarly, the areas of pain in our spiritual lives are the parts to which God wants to give special attention to make us healthier, more whole people.

The point of pain is the point of need. Many of us Christians go through the whole of our lives avoiding the point of pain. We constantly evade what Jesus is saying to us about a particular issue. He is saying to us,

'I can't really bless you and you can't really move on in the Christian life until you let me deal with that point of pain, because it is a crucial issue in your life. For years I've been telling you to do this, or to stop doing that, and you haven't obeyed me. You repeatedly back away from it because confronting it would be so painful for you. But you must bear the pain, because this problem needs to be sorted out.'

Often the point of pain will be something that makes us angry. That was certainly true of the Sanhedrin members: the things Jesus was doing made them angry. When God challenges people and they refuse to respond, they often become angry. The Sanhedrin members had locked themselves up in boxes with party labels. Nothing and no-one could penetrate those boxes. As a result they were useless to God: far worse than useless in fact, since they actively worked against God's own Son and in the end had a hand in crucifying him. People who lock themselves up in theological boxes, refusing to listen to anything new which God might be saying, refusing to listen to anything which challenges their security, refusing to let God touch their point of pain, are bound to be ineffective for God, since they will miss out on his truth and power.

It is interesting to note that the Sanhedrin members were saying amongst themselves, *'Here is this man performing many miraculous signs'* (verse 47). They didn't say, 'The people believe Jesus is performing miracles, but, of course, they are being conned; they are not real miracles, just conjuring tricks.' Even the enemies of Jesus recognized that he was doing real miracles. In those days there were plenty of charlatans around performing magic tricks, like Simon the sorcerer (Acts chapter 8). But the Sanhedrin members did not try to pretend that Jesus was one of them: his miracles were too powerful to be doubted, and too many people had witnessed them. So they knew Jesus was doing real miracles, but they didn't want to face up to the implications, that he was the Son of God and that they should acknowledge him as such and hand their lives over to his lordship. It would have been too costly for them, so they simply dodged the issue.

An unwitting prophet

Then one of them, named Caiaphas, who was high priest that year, spoke up, 'You know nothing at all! You do not realise that it is better for you that one man die for the people than that the whole nation perish.'

He did not say this on his own, but as high priest that year he prophesied that Jesus would die for the Jewish nation, and not only for that nation but also for the scattered children of God, to bring them together and make them one.

(John 11:49–52)

These are fascinating verses. Caiaphas thought he was just saying that they should have Jesus killed in order to prevent the Romans cracking down on the whole nation and destroying what freedom and stability they still had. But in fact, because he was serving as the high priest that year, he was being used by God to prophesy that Jesus, the Son of God, would die as a sacrifice for the sins of the nation and of all mankind; through the death of the one God–man, the whole world would have the opportunity to have eternal life in him.

Chapter 9

Responding to Jesus

Six days before the Passover, Jesus arrived at Bethany, where Lazarus lived, whom Jesus had raised from the dead. Here a dinner was given in Jesus' honour. Martha served, while Lazarus was among those reclining at the table with him. Then Mary took about a pint of pure nard, an expensive perfume; she poured it on Jesus' feet and wiped his feet with her hair. And the house was filled with the fragrance of the perfume.

But one of his disciples, Judas Iscariot, who was later to betray him, objected, 'Why wasn't this perfume sold and the money given to the poor? It was worth a year's wages.' He did not say this because he cared about the poor but because he was a thief; as keeper of the money bag, he used to help himself to what was put into it.

'Leave her alone,' Jesus replied. 'It was intended that she should save this perfume for the day of my burial. You will always have the poor among you, but you will not always have me.'

Meanwhile a large crowd of Jews found out that Jesus was there and came, not only because of him but also to see Lazarus, whom he had raised from the dead. So the chief priests made plans to kill Lazarus as well, for on account of him many of the Jews were going over to Jesus and putting their faith in him.

(John 12:1–11)

The pace of John's Gospel quickens at this point. We are moving rapidly to the climax of the ministry of Jesus – his death and resurrection. So significant is this that John takes almost half his gospel to discuss the events surrounding the cross. The first eleven chapters cover almost three years, the last ten chapters cover less than ten days!

John chapter 12 has four main sections: an act of love and devotion, a triumphant parade, a prophecy about the death of Jesus, and an example of stubborn unbelief.

Love and devotion

I have three children, all of whom are like Janet or me, in one way or another. But they are also very different from each other. They need, for example, to be disciplined using very different punishments. What works wonderfully for Sam may simply produce even worse behaviour in one of the girls. Just when you think you have got this whole parenting business sorted out, along comes the next child to prove you wrong!

Mary and Martha's parents must have been surprised at how different their daughters turned out to be. Sisters? Yes! but 'chalk and cheese' come to mind when you look at their actions and priorities (*cf.* Luke 10:38–42).

Less than a week before the Passover Jesus arrives back in Bethany for a special celebration dinner, held in his honour. Lazarus joins his sisters at this feast and the party begins. Martha serves food and Mary takes some perfumed ointment, worth about a year's wages to an ordinary working man, and anoints the feet of Jesus. Judas objects to this because he was hoping to be able to sell the ointment for the disciples' expenses fund – and to take a little cut for himself without anyone knowing!

Jesus knows that Judas is only faking a concern for

the poor and makes the pointed suggestion that Judas ought to look to the needs of his master in the few days he has left, and then he can devote a lifetime to helping the poor! They both know that this is not part of the Judas 'career plan'.

At first sight, Mary's action seems rather a waste, but it should be seen in the context of a woman who was overwhelmed with love for Jesus and gratitude to him for giving her brother the gift of life. Beyond duty, beyond obedience, beyond even service, there is love and adoration. Mary is overwhelmed. We often act as if we are underwhelmed! We go to church, attend our home group and give money to God's work ... but sometimes even these good things can hide a coldness, a dryness in our spirits. Oh to be 'lost in wonder, love and praise' as Mary was!

And Mary is not the only focus of attention in this story. Lazarus arouses a good deal of interest (verse 9). It's not every day that you can see a man who used to be dead! So powerful is the presence of Lazarus, that the religious leaders have him on their 'death list' as well as Jesus. Because of him many were putting their trust in Jesus.

When Jesus works in someone's life, especially in such a dramatic way, the impact can be enormous. One changed life can be the 'trigger' which releases lots of others to find God. I remember the minister of the church where I grew up telling a very moving story of a Durham mining village where a friend of his was sent as a pastor. The little chapel was really struggling with poor attendance and low morale. One day, after months of seemingly fruitless ministry, the pastor read the verses in John 12 about Lazarus. He felt constrained to cry to God in prayer: 'Lord, give me a Lazarus'. A few days later the biggest rogue in the village appeared at the back of an evangelistic service ... and was soundly converted! The whole village was staggered at the 'death to life' transformation of this man. When he gave his testimony some weeks later the chapel was packed, and others decided to follow this Jesus. From this point on, the church began to flourish.

The power of personal testimony is immense. A humble, simple explanation of what God has done in our lives can be effective where even the most carefully prepared evangelistic message fails. People who come to meet Fiona Castle, the widow of the well known and much loved Christian entertainer, Roy Castle, are sometimes surprised to end up meeting Jesus! And even the most anonymous Christian, even with an undramatic story can be effective. People may not be interested in Jesus, but they are interested in other people. Let's tell our story, privately and publicly, so what was said about Lazarus is said about us: ... *on account of him many were going over to Jesus and putting their faith in him.*

A triumphant parade

The next day the great crowd that had come for the Feast heard that Jesus was on his way to Jerusalem. They took palm branches and went out to meet him, shouting,

'Hosanna!'

'Blessed is he who comes in the name of the Lord!'

'Blessed is the King of Israel!'

Jesus found a young donkey and sat upon it, as it is written,

'Do not be afraid, O Daughter of Zion;
see, your king is coming,
seated on a donkey's colt.'

At first his disciples did not understand all this. Only after Jesus was glorified did they realise that these things had been written about him and that they had done these things to him.

Now the crowd that was with him when he called Lazarus from the tomb and raised him from the dead continued to spread the word. Many people, because they heard that he had given this miraculous sign, went out to meet him. So the Pharisees said to one another, 'See, this is getting us nowhere. Look how the whole world has gone after him!'

Now there were some Greeks among those who went up to worship at the Feast. They came to Philip, who was from Bethsaida in Galilee, with a request. 'Sir,' they said, 'we would like to see Jesus.' Philip went to tell Andrew; Andrew and Philip in turn told Jesus.

(John 12:12–22)

All four gospels record this important event. Jesus is moving ever nearer to his date with destiny in Jerusalem. What an exciting scene of celebration and joy John describes. The crowd had 'Passover fever' – the holiday feast is here! To add to the festive mood Jesus hits town and the word on the street hints at his kingship; is an uprising against the Romans in the offing? Palm branches are waved and shouts of joy fill the air on this very first Jesus March!

'Save us', they cry (Hosanna!) and shout Psalm 118:25, 26 and Zechariah 9:9 in his honour. For a few brief moments Roman oppression is forgotten as the King arrives. Somehow they all miss the significance of the donkey. The power of Jesus is not the human, political and military power of a conquering king, usually arriving on a thoroughbred stallion. This is the humble servant-king on a half-grown donkey.

In a power-crazy world this is an important reminder of how God views power. Even in the church, we can be tempted to believe in the power of the pound, the D. Mark or the dollar, and the superiority of political clout over prayer. True power is found in weakness, empowered by God. Perhaps it is worth meditating on Henry Milman's old hymn to understand how weakness can lead to 'triumph', 'power' and 'reigning'!

> Ride on! ride on in majesty!
> In lowly pomp ride on to die!
> O Christ, your triumphs now begin
> to capture death and conquer sin.
>
> Ride on! ride on in majesty!
> In lowly pomp ride on to die!
> Bow down your head to mortal pain,
> then take, O God, your power and reign!

As usual, the disciples caught on to the significance of this event, only after Jesus had left them (*cf.* Luke 24:25). It's such joy to me when the disciples seem to miss the significance of something Jesus says or does. There is hope for me after all! And I hope it's an encouragement for all of us to 'hang in there' when our progress in Christian understanding seems painfully slow. Peter was a classic example of this 'did not understand' problem (verse 16). He either doesn't get the point at all (Matthew 16:22), misses the main point (Mark 9:5) or gets the point, but is too cowardly to put it into practice (John 18:17)! Yet look how God used him (*e.g.* Acts 2:14; 3:6).

Let's keep on working hard at growing in our understanding of Jesus. Studying the Bible, even when we find it hard going; not missing church, even when it seems tedious; praying, even when we feel 'dry' and God seems deaf!

The religious leaders of the day certainly do feel like giving up (verse 19). There appears to be a mass rebellion against their control and a repudiation of their teaching. Fortunately, for them, they have temporarily forgotten how fickle public opinion is. Within days the adoring crowd will be baying for Jesus' life (19:15).

Not everyone who claims to follow Jesus and names him as King (*cf.* verse 13) has made a permanent pledge of allegiance to him. Sometimes in the emotion of a Christian gathering or because the people around us make certain responses, we are swept along on a wave of euphoria. But when a crisis comes faith can be tested. Warm feelings are not enough to carry us through disasters. This is one of the reasons that our evangelism should emphasize the cost of discipleship, as well as the benefits. Jesus must be followed because it is right, not because it is exciting; because of what he gave, not because of what I may get. He will nerve us for the battles we must fight, but does not remove us from the conflict.

What follows in verses 20–22, opens this whole episode up to a wider audience than simply the Jews. Some Greeks approach Philip, perhaps because he has a Greek name, wanting to meet Jesus. John is alerting us to the fact that the coming events have more than simply a Jewish significance: the death and resurrection of Jesus will affect the whole world. Their simple request (verse 21) has become the cry of all true seekers after truth. It is also the phrase which in past decades was used to challenge preachers. In recent years, and particularly in my year as President of the Baptist Union, I have visited hundreds of churches. Many of them have the phrase these Greeks used carved into the wall at the front of the church or displayed in the pulpit. It is a healthy reminder to all who preach and teach about the vital goal of our presentations. If people don't get to meet Jesus through what we say, we are short-changing them – however brilliant, funny or 'powerful' it may appear to us!

The death of Jesus prophesied

My son Samuel took a long time coming. My wife seemed to be in labour for ever. I felt utterly helpless to speed things up; and I hated to watch her discomfort. Finally, at a minute past midnight, Sam emerged into the world. After more than nine months, followed by another strenuous twenty hours, the moment all this had been leading up to, arrived. Without this moment, all that led up to it would have been pointless. In this next section we see Jesus arriving right on the edge of the moment his whole life had been leading up to – his hour has come!

Jesus replied, 'The hour has come for the Son of man to be glorified. I tell you the truth, unless a grain of wheat falls to the ground and dies, it remains only a single seed. But if it dies, it produces many seeds. The man who loves his life will lose it, while the man who hates his life in this world will keep it for eternal life. Whoever serves me must follow me; and where I am, my servant also will be. My Father will honour the one who serves me.

'Now my heart is troubled, and what shall I say? "Father, save me from this hour"? No, it was for this very reason I came to this hour. Father, glorify your name!'

Then a voice came from heaven, 'I have glorified it, and will glorify it again.' The crowd that was there and heard it said it had thundered; others said an angel had spoken to him.

Jesus said, 'This voice was for your benefit, not mine. Now is the time for judgment on this world; now the prince of this world will be driven out. But I, when I am lifted up from the earth, will draw all men to myself.' He said this to show the kind of death he was going to die.

The crowd spoke up, 'We have heard from the law that the Christ will remain for ever, so how can you say, "The Son of Man must be lifted up"? Who is this "Son of Man"?'

Then Jesus told them, 'You are going to have the light just a little while longer. Walk while you have the light, before darkness overtakes you. The man who walks in the dark does not know where he is going. Put your trust in the light while you have it, so that you may become sons of light.' When he had finished speaking, Jesus left and hid himself from them.

(John 12:23–36)

With the praise of the triumphal parade fading into the distance, Jesus becomes more solemn as he expresses the sober truth of his impending death. Using an analogy taken from local agriculture, he explains how death must come before life – both for him and his followers. This radical teaching has caused many people to give up their Christian faith or to shrink back from adopting it in the first place. Dying to our ambitions, pleasures, goals, dreams and 'agendas' is immensely painful, but it opens the door to an abundant life which nothing can surpass.

His imminent death was causing Jesus terrible stress (verse 27). It may shock us to realize that he was so troubled and upset. Surely God's Son could draw on his Father's resources to help him? Well, yes, but he was fully human as well as fully divine. He experienced our fears and anxieties – yet still acted in obedience (Hebrews 4:15). I'm so glad we don't have a God who is aloof, distant and detached from our feelings; but One who understands and weeps with us.

> When I am crushed in deep despair,
> When all against me rise,
> When every sinew's bound by care
> He understands my cries.
>
> When waves of sorrow o'er me roll,
> When hope within me dies,
> When hell itself weighs on my soul,
> He understands and cries!

Jesus can't bring himself to ask to be rescued from his predicament (verse 27:*cf.* Mark 14:36), because he knows that this death will mean life for him and countless others. Above everything else he wants glory to be given to his Father (verse 28). This was the 'secret of success' for Jesus. What we want most seems to change as we grow older. A baby wants to be held, young people want happiness, the middle-aged want health and the elderly, hope. Whatever our stage in life, the 'secret of success' is to want God's glory above everything!

Jesus then hears a voice affirming him in his prayer, just as he heard God speak at the start of his ministry (verses 28, 29: *cf.* Matthew 3:17). This voice signals the judgment of God on the world and the defeat of Satan – all accomplished through the cross (verses 32, 33). Sometimes we forget that the cross of Jesus dealt Satan a fatal blow. The way some people talk about the devil you'd think he was just as powerful as Jesus or that Jesus might just be able to beat him after a huge struggle; a points win, after the fight has gone the distance! The Bible does not support this view. The devil is given his marching orders (verse 31) by the cross. No ifs, buts or maybes. His defeat is certain. It's strange isn't it? What looks like a defeat for Jesus – his death – ends up being a defeat for the devil. What the Jews thought would bring a curse (verse 33: *cf.* Deuteronomy 21:23) turns out to bring a blessing on the whole world!

In the ancient world candles and torches provided most of the light, after dark. This made detailed, intricate work almost impossible after dusk; and it made travel after nightfall very hazardous. Jesus uses the fading light as a picture of time running out. 'I won't be around much longer, follow me while you can.' This note of urgency needs to affect our decisions and our evangelism. Tomorrow is not ours, only today is given to us. Too often we live as if we had all the time in the world.

> Said yesterday to to-morrow
> 'When I was young like you,
> I, too, was fond of boasting
> Of all I meant to do.
> But while I fell a-dreaming

Along the pleasant way,
Before I scarcely knew it,
I found it was to-day!

'And as to-day, so quickly
My little course was run,
I had not time to finish
One-half the things begun.
Would I could try it over
But I can ne'er go back
A yesterday forever,
I now must be, alack!

'And so, my good to-morrow,
If you would make a name
That history shall cherish
Upon its roll of fame,
Be all prepared and ready,
Your noblest part to play
In those new fleeting hours
When you shall be to-day.'

(anon)

Today is the day of salvation (2 Corinthians 6:2). This is the moment to be obedient to what God is saying to us. We must hold back no longer!

Stubborn unbelief

Even after Jesus had done all these miraculous signs in their presence, they still would not believe in him. This was to fulfil the word of Isaiah the prophet:

'Lord, who has believed our message
and to whom has the arm of the Lord been revealed?'

For this reason they could not believe, because, as Isaiah says elsewhere:
'He has blinded their eyes
and deadened their hearts,

so they can neither see with their eyes,
nor understand with their hearts,
nor turn – and I would heal them.'

Isaiah said this because he saw Jesus' glory and spoke about him.

Yet at the same time many even among the leaders believed in him. But because of the Pharisees they would not confess their faith for fear they would be put out of the synagogue; for they loved praise from men more than praise from God.

Then Jesus cried out, 'When a man believes in me, he does not believe in me only, but in the one who sent me. When he looks at me, he sees the one who sent me. I have come into the world as a light, so that no-one who believes in me should stay in darkness!

As for the person who hears my words but does not keep them, I do not judge him. For I did not come to judge the world, but to save it. There is a judge for the one who rejects me and does not accept my words; that very word which I spoke will condemn him at the last day. For I did not speak of my own accord, but the Father who sent me commanded me what to say and how to say it. I know that his command leads to eternal life. So whatever I say is just what the Father has told me to say.'

(John 12:37–50)

Some people just won't believe! Give them some compelling intellectual evidence, demonstrate how it changes lives and throw in some miracles ... and still they won't follow Jesus. These Jews seemed to have a callous over their spirits, hardened to Jesus and his message. Just as Isaiah had prophesied (Isaiah 53:1; 6:10), not everyone would find Jesus appealing, and some would come to despise and hate him.

We ought to remember this when we get involved in evangelism. Some will respond positively, some will simply ignore the message and others will react angrily and negatively. We must not be surprised by this or be put off from further evangelism. Many fine Christians did not react well to the Christian message the first time they heard it. Our job is to be faithful to the message; God can handle whatever response people choose to make.

Even in this cynical sea of unbelief, there are some signs of hope (verse 42). Jewish leaders turned to Jesus. Perhaps Nicodemus and Joseph of Arimathea were among them. Yet such was the stranglehold which the Pharisees had on the community, even leaders were scared to confess their faith publicly. John denounces such weakness strongly, but with a hint of sadness (verse 43). How easy it is to do what pleases other people, rather than be focused on pleasing God. For one thing, we think we will have to face other people today but won't have to face God until judgment day! Many of us hope he will have bigger things on his mind than our small lives when this moment arrives.

While we have sympathy for these Jewish leaders, we ought to recall that a great number of Christians only accomplished what they did in the kingdom of God, in the face of opposition from others. A desire to please God over-rode the natural desire to please their colleagues, friends or the community around them. Most of his contemporaries thought William Carey, 18th century missionary and founder of the Baptist Missionary Society, was mad to go to India, and even madder to stay! Month after month he faced criticism and opposition ... and had to wait seven years before Krishna Pal became the first convert. Later, Adoniram Judson was consistently opposed during his missionary work in Burma; even the believers back in England urged his return. On one occasion he wrote to them:

> Beg the churches to have patience. If a ship were here to carry me to any part of the world, I would not leave my field. Tell the brethren success is as certain as the promise of a faithful God can make it.

And the converts came. God-pleasers turn the world upside down! (*Cf.* Acts 4:19.)

When you believe in Jesus you believe in God (verse 44: *cf.* John 14:1) – a truly remarkable statement. Without a trace of pride Jesus declares his divinity. There is no boasting, no air of superiority, just an unadorned statement of fact. The Jesus who is God came primarily to bring salvation and speaks with supreme authority because he and his Father are in complete agreement about what to say (verse 49). This 'joint' message brings eternal life (verse 50). It's the most important message ever delivered, by the most significant person in history and our response to it is the most significant decision we will ever make!

Chapter 10

Love one another

It was just before the Passover Feast. Jesus knew that the time had come for him to leave this world and go to the Father. Having loved his own who were in the world, he now showed them the full extent of his love.

The evening meal was being served, and the devil had already prompted Judas Iscariot, son of Simon, to betray Jesus. Jesus knew that the Father had put all things under his power, and that he had come from God and was returning to God; so he got up from the meal, took off his outer clothing, and wrapped a towel round his waist. After that, he poured water into a basin and began to wash the disciples' feet, drying them with the towel that was wrapped round him.

(John 13:1–5)

The Servant King

For those of us who have been Christians for quite a few years the theme of Christian love can become somewhat over-familiar. We will have heard many sermons on this subject, and so we are tempted to let our minds wander when someone talks about it, thinking that we already know all there is to know about it. But John's teaching on love in chapter 13 is so powerful that we should all pay careful attention to it. The love which Jesus demonstrates here is so deep and so meaningful that all the words in the world cannot express it fully. Only as we follow Jesus' example do we begin to understand his love. The love of Jesus is not just a vague feeling of goodwill towards other people, and it is not just trying to be nice to each other: Jesus wants his love to grip our whole being and revolutionize our lives. The love of Jesus is about actions, not just words and feelings.

The action takes place in the Upper Room, where Jesus and the disciples were gathered together for the Last Supper before Jesus was arrested and crucified. They were all eating their meal, and during it Jesus got up and washed their feet. He took off his outer clothing to do this, which was how a slave would have done it. By this he was making himself a servant to the disciples. He had taken off his bodily clothes and had instead clothed himself with humility, in the words of 1 Peter 5:5. When Peter wrote those words he may well have been thinking of this incident, when Jesus made himself a servant to his disciples.

In the ancient world in hot climates like Palestine foot-washing was a regular custom. When people walked from one place to another their feet and legs used to get dusty and dirty, and on entering someone's house they would have their feet washed. In richer homes a servant would perform this task, and in ordinary homes the husband or wife would do it for the guests. The Upper Room was rented; there was no householder to wash the feet of the disciples, so Jesus did it. They were reclining at the table, and it would have been unpleasant for them to have each other's dirty feet near their faces, so Jesus volunteered to perform the lowly task of washing their feet. Although he was the leader of the group, he acted as a servant to them. He was not only their leader, he was the Son of God, and yet he humbled himself in this way. This is echoed in Philippians 2:7, where Paul writes that Jesus *made himself nothing, taking the very nature of a servant.* By this action Jesus was saying to the disciples, 'I don't stand on my status as the Son of God; I don't expect to be served by you – rather, I will serve you. I will do this job because anyone could do it. Status is not important to me. What is important is that you understand that I really love you and care for you, so much so that I am not bothered about my reputation.'

By taking this attitude Jesus was turning the contemporary Jewish conventions upside down. The Jews had a very clear pecking order. Of course, men were always dominant, and women always came last. And among men it was always the oldest who had the most status. The youngest disciple was probably the one who, according to the customs of the day, ought to have washed everyone's feet. Perhaps the disciples had been arguing about who was the most junior among them, since they were all unwilling to do the menial, unpleasant task. So Jesus took this opportunity to show the disciples that status is not important.

Some of us are more obsessed with status than others, but all of us care about it to some degree: we want to be respected and liked, we want our talents and achievements to be recognized and appreciated. Frankly, some of us enjoy being in positions of power because we have a psychological need to dominate and control other people. But the gospel of Jesus cuts right across all of that. The crucial issue is not who is most important or who is of the most value or who is in charge: what matters is that we should love one another. In a sense, status has been abolished in the church. Of course, the church needs people to lead it, but that leadership is not based on status: in the church those in leadership are not more important than those who are following them. Christian leadership is meant to be *servant-leadership.* A Christian leader is primarily the servant of the people whom he or she leads. Indeed, the very word 'minister' is a Latin word which literally means 'servant'. Christian leadership is only valid and truly effective when it is servant-leadership; if it is status-leadership it is not leadership based on the pattern set by the Lord Jesus. His own leadership was a million miles away from the kind of attitude which wants a position of status in order to dominate and control other people. Graham Kendrick's popular worship song 'The Servant King' expresses very well the truth that although Jesus was the Son of God, the Heavenly King, he was also the servant of his followers. Indeed, he gave far more of himself than most servants ever do: he gave his very life for us. Leaders in the church must be motivated by love for those they lead: their desire should be to serve them, to care for them, to bless them, to enable them to grow, to help them to develop their God-given talents.

This passage in John's Gospel is not just a word to leaders but to all Christians. The example which Jesus gave us in this incident shows us the importance of putting others before ourselves. He didn't wash his own feet: he washed everyone else's. Perhaps the disciples were so embarrassed that afterwards one of them washed his feet too. John doesn't tell us.

Hasty Peter

Peter was shocked by the sight of Jesus washing the disciples' feet. When it was his turn he said in amazement,

'Lord, are you going to wash my feet?' Jesus replied, 'You do not realise now what I am doing, but later you will understand.'

(verses 6–7)

He had not yet realized that Jesus had come to be a servant and that he wanted all his followers to do the same. Peter was still thinking in worldly terms: he thought leadership was about being served by other people rather than serving them.

Throughout the gospels we see Peter opening his mouth rashly and immediately regretting it. At the transfiguration, after he had seen Jesus talking with Moses and Elijah, he said,

'Lord, it is good for us to be here. If you wish, I will put up three shelters—one for you, one for Moses and one for Elijah.'
(Matthew 17:4)

It had been a wonderful experience and Peter wanted to preserve and prolong it. For a simple, impulsive man, it was an understandable response, but they could not stay for ever on the mountain; they had to go back down into the hurly-burly of human society (see Matthew 17:1–13).

Peter is a very likeable character, because although he was rash and clumsy, he was also absolutely committed. Whatever he said, he really meant. He was often slow to understand what Jesus was teaching him, but once he had got the message there was no stopping him: he became the proverbial bull in a china shop. With Peter it was all or nothing. That was probably why Jesus chose him to be the 'Rock' on which to build his church, since nothing short of death would ever be able to stop him from proclaiming the gospel which Jesus had taught him.

Here in the Upper Room Peter foolishly said to Jesus,

'No ... you shall never wash my feet.' Jesus answered, 'Unless I wash you, you have no part with me.'

Peter did not understand that Jesus was talking about his own servanthood; Peter's reply to Jesus was,

'Then Lord, ... not just my feet but my hands as well!'

In other words, 'Let's have a bath!' Jesus then said,

'A person who has had a bath needs only to wash his feet; his whole body is clean.'

(verses 8–10)

He was saying, 'Peter, don't get carried away. You don't understand what I'm saying. I'm not trying to give you a bath: you had a bath before you came here. It's just that your feet are dirty because of the dust on the streets, and by washing them I wanted to show you that I love you and that I am willing to be your servant.'

And more than that, Jesus wanted to show the disciples that they should also serve one another.

When he had finished washing their feet, he put on his clothes and returned to his place. 'Do you understand what I have done for you?' he asked them. 'You call me "Teacher" and "Lord", and rightly so, for that is what I am. Now that I, your Lord and Teacher, have washed your feet, you also should wash one another's feet. I have set you an example that you should do as I have done for you.'

(verses 12–15)

If their Lord and Teacher (or Rabbi, literally 'honoured one') had humbled himself and washed their feet, then surely they should wash one another's feet.

In some denominations, particularly in the USA, people practise foot-washing today as part of their expression of the Christian faith. Often they do it just before Communion, and they find that because the foot-washing symbolizes their love for one another and their willingness to serve one another it makes the Communion much more meaningful to them. Usually foot-washing is practised in small congregations: it is hard to imagine how a large church could do it, it would take all Sunday! Foot-washing is not something which Jesus has commanded us to do as a regular part of the life of the church, like Communion, but it is a beautiful expression of Christian love.

By washing the disciples' feet Jesus was showing us that we should put aside all concerns about status: we should not consider any job in the church as too lowly for us. When we have been church members for some years there is a tendency for us to think that we have got beyond certain things, like making the coffee or sweeping the floor or coping with difficult people; we think that such things are for other, more junior church members. But Jesus is saying to us that that is worldly thinking which has no place in the church: we are all servants of one another, even leaders of the church.

By this incident and by his whole life Jesus showed us that love is not just a feeling: real love means *action.* In the English language the word 'love' has become very debased. We say we 'love' a certain kind of food, or we 'love' a particular pastime. 'Love' can mean a teen-ager's gooey feelings for a girl or boy at school. But real Christian love – the kind of love which Jesus demon-strated in his life – always honours and affirms the loved one and finds expression in loving actions. Jesus didn't just have kind feelings towards his disciples; he showed them that he loved them by performing for them the simple and lowly task of washing their dirty feet. Love is an *action*: it means reaching out to other people and doing something which blesses them.

Betrayal

Jesus had been eating a meal with his friends, and ordinarily this would have been a happy occasion; but Jesus was sorrowful.

Jesus was troubled in spirit and testified, 'I tell you the truth, one of you is going to betray me.'

(verse 21)

Jesus often knew things supernaturally: he knew things which, humanly speaking, it was not possible for him to have known in advance. Sometimes this was because he was the Son of God: he knew God's thoughts because he himself was God. We shall never have that kind of divine knowledge. But sometimes Jesus knew secret things because he was a man walking in complete harmony with God. He was so closely in touch with God, his human spirit was so in tune with God's Spirit, that he knew what God was thinking and feeling.

This is a closeness to God which we too can experience to some degree. We can pray that we shall have the same sensitivity that Jesus had. By God's Spirit we can react as God reacts to the things which are going on in the world and in our lives. We can feel something of what God feels about the wars, the famines, the cruelties and oppressions in the world. We can know what God thinks about the sin in the world, and the sin in our own lives. Knowing God's heart can be a joyful thing: we can feel his joy and the joy of the angels in heaven when people become Christians. But we can also feel the pain which the sin of the world causes him. If people's inhumanity to each other distresses us, how much more does it distress God, the Creator of all people? If, for example, we are sickened by the crimes of a mass murderer, how must those crimes appal God, who created the murderer? Having the spiritual sensitivity which Jesus had is something which we should not take lightly: it is a very serious matter to know God's thoughts and feelings. We should think very carefully before praying for it.

Because of this closeness to God Jesus knew that Judas Iscariot was about to betray him, and this distressed him greatly. We can only begin to imagine how Jesus must have felt about it. For three years he had lived in the company of this man, counting him one of his friends, and now Judas was going to betray him. To say that Jesus felt deeply hurt by this is an understatement. Jesus told Judas,

'What you are about to do, do quickly' ... As soon as Judas had taken the bread, he went out. And it was night.

(verses 27, 30)

It was literally night-time, but it was also night in Judas's heart. His soul had become darker than we can imagine. What a terrible thing, to go down in history as the man who betrayed the Son of God!

All Christians feel appalled by what Judas did: we love the Lord Jesus and we feel that to betray him was utterly despicable. None of us have betrayed Jesus in quite so literal a manner as Judas did, but we all betray him to varying degrees by the sin in our lives. Often we do not follow him with complete loyalty and faithfulness. It is an easy thing to go to church on a Sunday to worship God, and to talk with our Christian friends about how wonderful the gospel is and how good God has been to us, but it is not easy to be a consistent Christian witness at our place of work or with our neighbours who have no time for God. Often, in subtle ways, we betray Jesus by failing to witness for him, by failing to behave as one of his disciples should. If our behaviour on a Monday morning is markedly different from the way we act on a Sunday, we are betraying Jesus. We have no justification for pointing an accusing finger at Judas Iscariot, because all of us, no matter how long we have been Christians, have moments of betrayal, moments when we are just a little bit ashamed to admit that we are followers of Jesus, when we keep silent in order to avoid the mocking or hostility of our workmates or neighbours or family.

It is sobering to reflect that Judas was probably not an obviously wicked person. He was a member of Jesus' team of disciples for three years. If he had been an obnoxious, difficult, immoral, evil person, Jesus could not have tolerated his presence: he would have been too disruptive an influence and would have had a bad effect on the other disciples. He probably seemed an average Jewish man of his time, with his good points and bad points just like all the other disciples. During the three years he had been constantly in the company of Jesus, the Son of God, he had witnessed Jesus' amazing miracles: he had seen him heal countless people and even raise folk from the dead; he had heard Jesus' wonderful teaching, both to the crowds and more intimately to the disciples. He had probably talked with Jesus one to one on many occasions. He had probably done miracles and healed the sick in the name of Jesus, as the other disciples had done. Judas probably knew and believed that Jesus was the Son of God. And yet, despite all this, he had ended up betraying Jesus. There will always be a measure of mystery about this betrayal. How could he possibly have done it? Why did he succumb to the devil's temptation to do this dreadful deed?

Judas's treachery is a warning to all Christians. Let us ensure that there is nothing in our lives which betrays or dishonours Jesus. We need to remember that Judas went through all the motions of being a disciple of Jesus, but there was still betrayal in his heart of hearts.

Commanded to love

After Judas had gone Jesus said to the remaining disciples,

'A new command I give you: Love one another. As I have loved you, so you must love one another. By this all men will know that you are my disciples, if you love one another.'

(verses 34–35)

The kind of love Jesus was talking about here was very different from romantic love. The classic romantic situation is where two young people meet and fall in love. They then spend days or weeks in a heightened emotional state, wandering around in a kind of daze. They don't sleep well or eat properly, and they can't concentrate on anything because they are constantly thinking of the beloved. That kind of emotional, romantic love is a beautiful part of human life, and I have no wish to knock it. But it is not the kind of love which Jesus was talking about. He *commanded* the disciples to love one another, and, obviously, we cannot summon up affectionate feelings for people just because we have been commanded to love them. No, the love which Jesus was talking about was not primarily to do with the emotions but to do with the *will*.

When people get married they make promises to God and to each other, committing themselves to love their partner until death separates them. Their marriage will have started with romantic love or perhaps just close friendship, but on their wedding day the couple commit themselves to love each other come what may. Every marriage has its ups and downs, and there are times when it is easy to love your partner, and others when it's not so easy! But if people have taken their marriage vows seriously, they will keep on loving each other through thick and thin, and when the difficult times are over they will still have a marriage. Emotion is part of marital love, but that love is also a matter of the will, of deliberate commitment. Without that commitment a marriage is unlikely to survive the trials and tribulations of normal marital and family life.

Love between Christians is somewhat like that. We are commanded by Jesus to love *all* of our brothers and sisters in Christ. In some cases this will be easy, because we like the people concerned; in other cases it will be difficult, because we don't like them. Indeed, they may be a real pain in the neck to us! But whether we like them or not, we still have to love them. That does not mean we have to try to crank up in ourselves nice, fraternal, warm feelings for everyone: what it does mean is committing ourselves to love them, no matter how hard we find it. Christian love is an act of the will: 'I *will* love them, even though they rub me up the wrong way, because Jesus has told me to do it; and to demonstrate that love I will be kind to them, I will do what I can to help them in practical ways, I will invite them around to dinner, even though there are plenty of people in the church whose company I would rather have …' Jesus did not tell us to *feel* love for people but to *be* loving to them and to *do* loving things for them. Jesus is saying to us, 'Love one another. I'm not asking you to like one another; I'm not even commanding you to get on well together, ands it's not a question of whether you think this or that person is nice. *Love them!*'

An act of the Holy Spirit

So Christian love is an act of the human will, but it is also an act of the Holy Spirit. Paul wrote,

God has poured out his love into our hearts by the Holy Spirit, whom he has given us.

(Romans 5:5)

Once we have decided to love someone, the Holy Spirit then begins to work in our heart and we may actually begin to *feel* his love for the person, and then we will start to like them as well, even if our natural inclination was to dislike them. But our decision to love must come first. And even if we never get to feel that we like some people, the Spirit of God will give us the strength and warmth to love them.

Thus the Christian church is completely different from any other social grouping. In other contexts people flock together because they like each other or they have a common interest. But the church is made up of all sorts of people with very different personalities, backgrounds and interests. We will like some (hopefully most) of the people in our local church, but there will always be some whom we do not naturally like. But with God's grace we can love them, and then eventually we will end up liking them as well. A church is not just a club of like-minded people who gather together. At the heart of their relationships with one another is a deep-seated, God-given love which nothing and no-one can destroy. Jesus told the disciples that their love for one another would be the proof that Christianity is real. He said,

'All men will know that you are my disciples, if you love one another.'

(verse 35)

In other words, the whole world will know that there is something revolutionary about Christians if they really love one another. The world looks at Christians, at the life of the church, and what they see will decide whether or not they are convinced that Jesus is real and alive today.

Do we really have this kind of love for one another, or is our 'love' little more than normal human politeness dressed up in 'Christian' guise? Do we really love people, even if we find them hard to like? Or do we pay lip service to the ideal of Christian love, but in practice snub or avoid the people we don't like or who have hurt us in some way?

Peter's promise

Peter rashly promised Jesus,

'I will lay down my life for you.'

Jesus replied, 'Will you really lay down your life for me? I tell you the truth, before the cock crows, you will disown me three times!'

(verses 37–38)

Jesus predicted that Peter, while not actually betraying

Jesus as Judas had done, would deny him when he was arrested and Peter's own position was precarious. There is a challenge in that for us today. We may say to God, 'Yes, I will love my brothers and sisters in Christ,' but when the going gets tough we may in effect deny this promise, saying to ourselves, 'After what he/she has done/said, I can't possibly be expected to love him/her!' Our commitment to love has to be more than a superficial promise, more than a matter of mere words; it has to be a commitment rooted in our inner being. Love must be not just a word on our lips but an action which dominates our lives.

Chapter 11

In my Father's house

> *'Do not let your hearts be troubled. Trust in God; trust also in me. In my Father's house are many rooms; if it were not so, I would have told you. I am going there to prepare a place for you. And if I go and prepare a place for you, I will come back and take you to be with me that you also may be where I am. You know the way to the place where I am going.'*
>
> (John 14:1–4)

Trusting the word of Jesus

Mark chapter 14 provides us with some illuminating background to John chapter 14. In Mark 14, just before the Lord's Supper, the disciples asked Jesus,

'Where do you want us to go and make preparations for you to eat the Passover?'

Jesus told the disciples to go into Jerusalem, where

'a man carrying a pot of water will meet you. Follow him. Say to the owner of the house he enters, "The Teacher asks: Where is my guest room, where I may eat the Passover with my disciples?" He will show you a large upper room, furnished and ready. Make preparations there.'

The disciples left, went into the city and found things just as Jesus had told them. So they prepared the Passover.

It may be that Jesus knew all these specific details

because he was God and so had God's foreknowledge. That is one of the possible explanations: no mere human could predict such things so accurately. And John chapters 13 and 14 took place immediately after this incident, so this amazing case of Jesus' God-given foreknowledge must have been fresh in the disciples' minds. Knowing this, Jesus now told them about what was going to happen in the future – he must go to his father and he would then come back for his disciples. In effect he was saying to them, 'I told you exactly what would happen when you came into Jerusalem to find the Upper Room. Everything I told you was correct in every detail, wasn't it? I asked you to trust me about this small matter, and I am now asking you to trust me about a much more important matter. I was right about the small matter, and I am right about this greater matter too. I gave you specific instructions about this room, and I am now giving you specific promises about an eternity which is guaranteed in my name. Just as you relied on my words for this room in this house we are now in, rely on my words about the room in my Father's heavenly house. My word about the earthly room was true, and you will find that my word about the heavenly room is also true.'

Our human knowledge is limited. We know only about the present and the past: we cannot accurately predict the future. But God actually knows what the future will be like: he can see it, because he lives in eternity, not in the linear time-line in which we live. As Moses discovered in Exodus chapter 3, God is the great I AM: he exists in an eternal present. Past, present and future are all one to him. Hebrews 13:8 tells us that *Jesus Christ is the same yesterday and today and for ever.* God is the only person who knows what tomorrow will bring. This is very reassuring for us. The God who loves and cares for us knows exactly what will happen in the future. He knows what the future holds for all of us. So when Jesus, the Son of God, speaking with the foreknowledge of God, promises us that he has gone to prepare a place for us in his Father's heavenly house, we can be sure that what he says is true. We can be confident that our future is in his hands, and that in him we have complete security, complete assurance of salvation and eternal life.

Some commentators have viewed this account from a different angle. Perhaps Jesus knew all those details in advance precisely because he had made all the detailed arrangements himself. If this is so perhaps we should understand that the Lord who made careful preparations for the Last Supper is the same Lord who will prepare for our reception in heaven. This is another facet of the truth revealed in these verses.

Fear God, but don't be afraid

Jesus told the disciples, *'Do not let your hearts be troubled'* (verse 1), or, in other words, 'Let your minds be at peace. Do not worry. Do not be anxious or upset.' The disciples were sitting there in the Upper Room, panic-stricken by the thought that Jesus was going to leave them. They didn't understand where he was going, but he had told them he was going to be with them '*only a little longer*' (John 13:33). They were wondering anxiously who would replace Jesus as their leader. What should they do next? Who were they going to look to for security? Jesus told them not to worry, not to fear.

The Bible tells us two very important things about fear. On the one hand, it tells us not to be afraid about the future, about what is happening to us, about our jobs, our families, our basic needs such as food and clothing. But on the other hand Scripture tells us to *fear God.* The message of Scripture is that we have no need to be afraid of anything or anyone except God.

Why should we fear God? Because he is the great, awesome Creator of the universe, the Lord of heaven and earth, the King of Kings. He is a pure and holy God who will not tolerate sin. He is more powerful than we can possibly imagine. All the power of mankind – all the electricity we could generate in all the world's power stations – is as nothing compared to the power of the God who made this vast universe in which our earth is a tiny, insignificant speck of cosmic dust.

In the church in recent decades we have emphasized the fact that through Jesus we have a personal relationship with God. This is perfectly true, but sometimes that aspect of the biblical message has been so emphasized as to obscure the fact that the God with whom we have this relationship is the Almighty Creator of the universe, and we are merely his creations. Yes, on the one hand God is our friend, but on the other hand he is *God.* There is sometimes a tendency in churches today to be somewhat flippant and casual about God. We think of God as our pal, as the old man up in the sky with a white beard and an over-indulgent fondness for his children. I believe some modern Christians need to fear God much more than they do.

But how can we fear God, whom we are commanded to love? 'Fear' here means awe, respect for his power and reverence and wholesome humility in his presence. We do not need to be afraid of him as if he were an ogre.

If we do fear God, humbly putting our trust in him and handing our lives over to him, we need fear nothing else in all the world. I meet many Christians today who are oppressed by fear. Some people are afraid of the future and what it will bring. Some are afraid about what will become of their children, growing up in a world which is changing too rapidly and which seems to be disintegrating around our ears. Others are afraid for their elderly parents, concerned about the suffering they might have to endure in their old age. Many people are fearful about losing their jobs:

few professions have the job security they used to offer at one time. Many people are fearful about their health. The list of fears is almost endless. There are certainly plenty of things we can be afraid about in this life.

But from Genesis to Revelation the message of Scripture to us is *Do not be afraid!* Jesus has told us,

'Do not worry about your life, what you will eat or drink; or about your body, what you will wear ... Who of you by worrying can add a single hour to his life? ... Therefore do not worry about tomorrow, for tomorrow will worry about itself. Each day has enough trouble of its own.'

(Matthew 6:25, 27, 34)

Worrying accomplishes nothing: it cannot make us richer, healthier, taller, stronger, fitter, more intelligent, more beautiful, more popular. Instead of worrying we should trust God to provide everything we need. Of course, even though we know this, we still tend to worry anyway – it comes naturally to us and we seem to think we need to keep our hand in!

In Genesis God said to Abraham (or Abram, as he then was), 'Do not be afraid to leave the safety and security of your own country, people and family. Go to the land I will show you, and I will make your family into a nation more numerous than the grains of sand on the seashore or the stars in the heavens. Take your wife, your servants, your animals and all your possessions, and I will go with you' (see Genesis chapter 12). Throughout the Scriptures God is saying the same thing to his people: 'Do not be afraid; I am with you.'

And right at the end of the Bible, in the book of Revelation, the apostle John has an amazing vision of Jesus. Before Jesus' crucifixion and resurrection John had seen him eating, sleeping, talking with his friends, preaching the good news of the Kingdom, healing the sick ... but now he was seeing Jesus fully revealed as the Son of God in all his heavenly glory. Jesus was ...

dressed in a robe reaching down to his feet and with a golden sash round his chest. His head and hair were white like wool, as white as snow, and his eyes were like blazing fire. His feet were like bronze glowing in a furnace, and his voice was like the sound of rushing waters. In his right hand he held seven stars, and out of his mouth came a sharp double-edged sword. His face was like the sun in all its brilliance.

(Revelation 1:13–16)

John was so overcome by what he saw that he fell at Jesus' feet as *though dead*. But Jesus said to him,

'Do not be afraid, I am the First and the Last. I am the Living One; I was dead, and behold I am alive for ever and ever! And I hold the keys of death and Hades.'

(verses 17–18)

The Jesus who was now saying *'Do not be afraid'* was the same one who in the Upper Room had said, *'Do not let your hearts be troubled'*.

What Jesus was saying in John 14:1 was not, 'Cheer up! Everything will be all right. Stop looking so down in the mouth!' That is the most unhelpful sort of thing one can say to someone who is afraid and worried. Jesus was not offering platitudes and empty reassurances. He was telling the disciples not to be afraid because he was God and he was in charge of their lives. He was about to die for their salvation, and so he could guarantee them that their eternal destiny was absolutely secure in his hands. And what Jesus said then to the disciples he says to all Christians in all ages. We can rely on him totally for our salvation, knowing that we are safe in his divine, loving hands. We are not guaranteed physical safety – even Christians may have road accidents or fall ill – but our final destiny is secure.

From the general to the specific

Jesus told the disciples, *'Trust in God; trust also in me'* (John 14:1). The original Greek text is problematic here, so it is difficult to translate, but I believe that the NIV's footnote gives the best sense: *'You trust in God; trust also in me.'* Jesus was saying to them, 'I know that you trust in God. You are good Jews, and so you have been brought up to fear him and to obey his commandments. Now I am the Son of God; I am his personal representative on earth. So just as you have always trusted God, my Father, now trust me, his Son. Because I am his Son I am every bit as trustworthy as he is, because I share his character in every respect. God has never let you down, and neither will I, for I am God, I am Jesus: my name means "Saviour". To be the Saviour was the reason for my being born into the world. Trust in me, and you will be saved.'

The disciples needed to hear that, and the world today needs to hear it too. Many people have a vague, generalized belief in God. They sense that there is a Being who made everything and who rules the world; they believe there must be Something or Someone greater than ourselves. But there is a big difference between believing in God in this general way and believing in Jesus as one's personal Saviour. Jesus came into the world to make that general belief in God into a personal, specific salvation-event for each one of us. He came so that God would no longer be a distant figure but a personal God who transforms our lives. Jesus came to make God real to individual people.

A perfect home

Jesus told the disciples, *'In my Father's house are many rooms'* (verse 2). The old King James Version of the Bible had 'mansions' here instead of 'rooms', but the NIV's translation is much more accurate. Literally the Greek word translated 'rooms' means 'place of abiding' or 'home'. So in God the Father's heavenly house there are many homes.

The fact that there are many homes and not just a

limited number means that there is room in heaven for everyone who believes and trusts in Jesus. Heaven is not just for an elite, select few. Everyone who wants to get into heaven, who wants to know and love Jesus, will have a home there. Heaven is a very, very big place. The gate into heaven is narrow (see Matthew 7:13–14), that gate is Jesus himself, but heaven is a broad, spacious place. There is room in heaven for the whole of the human race, if they will accept Jesus as their Saviour. God does not wish to exclude anyone from heaven, as Peter tells us: '*He is patient with [us], not wanting anyone to perish, but everyone to come to repentance*' (2 Peter 3:9).

The fact that Jesus describes our place in heaven as a home is very significant. There is a big difference between a mere house and a home. People who have lived in student digs will clearly understand this point. A house is an arrangement of bricks and timber with a front door, a back door, windows and rooms. Materially a home is just the same as a house, but it has a vital extra ingredient. In student digs the young people may live in the same house, but if they are not already friends they tend to lead separate lives, even though they are living under the same roof. A home, on the other hand, is the place where a family or friends live. There is love and a sense of shared life there. Our place in heaven will be a home rather than a mere house: it will be a place where we belong, where we are part of a loving family.

The saying goes that an Englishman's home is his castle, and often we like to pull up the drawbridge to keep the rest of the world out. Our home is where we feel secure and at peace. Often after a day's work we are grateful to shut the door and forget all about the rest of the world until tomorrow morning. Our home is our bolt-hole where we can escape from the pressure and hassle of the workaday world. Heaven will be like that, only more so. In heaven all the insecurity, worry, pain, suffering, tears, sin and evil of the world will be shut out for ever, and we will never have to endure it again.

Of course, in an earthly home we can never experience that total peace because when we enter the home we bring our own sin into it. As a result earthly homes can be fraught with problems and conflict between people. But in our heavenly home we will all be perfect, sinless individuals: we will finally be free from our own sinfulness and the sinfulness of others. Consequently we shall experience perfect peace, security and happiness there. Nothing will be able to destroy the peace of heaven. Thieves will not be able to break into it and moth and rust will not be able to destroy it (see Matthew 6:20). Here and now we cannot know that peace in its fullness because we are still afflicted by the sin and corruption of the world, but if we trust in Jesus as our Saviour we know that heaven is our final destination. All Christians have to live in the tension between looking forward to the perfect peace of heaven and living in an imperfect world.

Jesus has told us, *'I am going there to prepare a place for you'* (verse 2). The wording in the Greek suggests two pictures to us. One of those images is that of a forerunner, the one who goes ahead to reconnoitre. When an army is advancing through unfamiliar territory it will send scouts on ahead to spy out the land and make sure that the way forward is clear and safe. The other picture is of someone who gets a house ready for someone else to live in. This is a very homely image. When my wife Jan and I moved from Preston in Lancashire to Stopsley in Luton back in the early eighties, we hired a three-ton lorry to transport most of our possessions, and a friend drove it down to Stopsley for us. I had to go to Norfolk to collect some of Jan's things, while Jan and our friend went to our new house. I was delayed in Norfolk and so arrived late, and by the time I arrived everything in the lorry had been shifted into the house! Our friend had already done all the unloading. As Christians we are not going to a place where a lot of work still needs to be done to make it habitable: Jesus has already gone on ahead and done all of that for us. He died on the cross, rose from the dead and went to be with his Father, and right now he is busy in the heavenly realms with his angels, preparing homes for you and me to live in. That's how much he loves us: he wants everything to be just right for us when we get there. I think that is a lovely, comforting picture: the Son of God arranging and preparing heavenly homes for us to live in.

Two guarantees

In verse 3 Jesus promises us two things:

'And if I go and prepare a place for you, I will come back and take you to be with me that you also may be where I am.'

First, he promised that he would come back. Jesus came down from heaven and was born into the world as a baby, lived his life, died for our sins, rose from the dead and went back to heaven. At the close of history he will once again come to earth to judge mankind and to take his children with him to heaven. He will step from eternity back into time, and all the people on earth will recognize him for who he is, and the world as we know it will come to an end.

We Christians need to live our daily lives in the knowledge that Jesus may come back at any time: it could be in a thousand years, or a century, or next year, or tomorrow. He has not told us when he will return but we know he will come back at some time. We need to remember that we may not necessarily live to the age of ninety-six or whatever: we may not have a whole life to live before Jesus returns. If he comes back before our physical death, all our plans about this life will suddenly become irrelevant. All the plans we make for our lives need to be provisional plans: 'We plan to do such and such, unless the Lord returns before then.'

Secondly, Jesus promised us that having come back, he would take us with him to heaven. The Bible does not give us many specific details about what heaven will be like. People get all sorts of strange ideas about it. When I was a teenager I didn't find the prospect of heaven very appealing, because I thought it would simply be one long church service! However, John 14:3 makes one thing very clear: in heaven we will be with Jesus. He said he would come back so that *'you also may be where I am'*. The most important thing we can know about heaven is that we shall be in the presence of Jesus there, and it is not possible to conceive of anything more wonderful, exciting, comforting and reassuring than that.

Sometimes when we are worshipping God, perhaps in church or in a home group or even in our personal prayer times, we get so caught up in it and so touched by the Holy Spirit that for a second or two, or perhaps longer, we are keenly aware of the presence of Jesus. It seems that he is right there with us, gladly receiving our worship and blessing us. We feel that we have been lifted up into heaven, just for a few moments. I believe that when we get to heaven, it will be a lot like that, only the experience of being in the presence of God will be far more powerful; it will also be permanent, not something that comes and goes and leaves us longing for it to be repeated or prolonged. In heaven we will enjoy a continuous, perfect, beautiful, overwhelming closeness to Jesus.

A narrow path

Jesus said:

'*... You know the way to the place where I am going.*'

Thomas said to him, 'Lord, we don't know where you are going, so how can we know the way?'

Jesus answered, 'I am the way and the truth and the life. No-one comes to the Father except through me.'

(John 14:4–6)

Thomas had in effect asked Jesus, 'What is the way to the place where you are going?' and Jesus had answered, 'I myself am the Way, I am your Way to God; I am the Truth about God; and I am the Life of God for you.' This is one of the great 'I am' sayings of Jesus. Elsewhere he says, *'I am the bread of life'* (John 6:35), *'I am the light of the world'* (8:12), *'I am the good shepherd'* (10:11, 14), *'I am the resurrection and the life'* (11:25), and here he says, *'I am the way and the truth and the life.'* In fact, in the Greek the words 'truth' and 'life' can be read as adjectives describing the noun 'way', so a better translation might be, 'I am the true and living way.'

Then Jesus said something very challenging, something which upsets many people: *'No-one comes to the Father except through me.'* That is an astonishing claim. It is either a true statement or a piece of amazing arrogance. We have to decide one way or the other. If it is true, we must accept Jesus as the only way to God. If it is not true, we cannot just safely consign Jesus to our personal collection of great moral and spiritual leaders, because we could not trust someone who made such a claim if it were not true. As C. S. Lewis pointed out, someone who makes the kind of statements about himself that Jesus made must be either God or mad or bad. You can't avoid the choice.

This is where the Christian message bites at its hardest. In one sense Christianity is as broad as the world: Jesus hangs there on the cross for us and says, 'Anyone who wants eternal life can have it: all you have to do is believe in me as your Saviour. I will turn no-one away: everyone is welcome, from every age in history, every colour, race, creed, culture, whatever your sins, whatever your intelligence or lack of it.' But in another sense the gospel is a very narrow message, because Jesus also says, 'To have this eternal life you must come through *me.* No-one else will do; no other person can save you from your sins, because I am the only Saviour there has ever been or ever will be.'

This offends many people today. They argue that all religions lead to God, and that it is arrogant of Christians to claim that Jesus is the only way. But if we take the Word of God seriously, we have no choice but to say that Jesus is the only way, because he himself said it: '*No-one comes to the Father except through me.*' Now, of course, that does not mean that the other religions and philosophies in the world are total nonsense and utterly worthless. There is moral, spiritual and philosophical truth in all of them: in the world's religions and philosophies we see mankind trying to understand themselves and the world and God, and some of the insights which they achieve are of value. However, the only way to be saved from our sins, the only way to eternal life, the only way into the presence of God, is through Jesus Christ. So when Jesus said, '*No-one comes to the Father except through me,*' he was making a take-it-or-leave-it statement: the matter was simply not open for discussion. He told us the truth, and we have to make a simple choice: to accept it or reject it.

Frequently Christians are accused of arrogance because they make this claim about Jesus. Sometimes that charge of arrogance is not altogether unjustified, as Christians may present the gospel in a proud, condescending manner. We must tell people that Jesus is the only way to God, because that is the plain truth and they need to hear it. But we must speak that message with gentleness and humility, conscious that the only difference between us and the people we are talking to is that we are saved sinners and they are as yet unsaved sinners; we should not speak with arrogance, enjoying the fact that we are right and they are wrong.

Life can be likened to a huge quagmire through which just one narrow path leads to safety on the other side. If we follow any path except this one we will end up getting stuck in the clinging mud of the bog. Jesus Christ is the path: only by accepting him as the Way can we safely reach the presence of God. So the Way into heaven is very narrow – it is Jesus and Jesus only – but once we have found that Way, once we have accepted Jesus as our Lord and Saviour, the whole of the universe becomes available to us as God blesses us with every spiritual blessing in Christ.

What about those who have never heard?

This is a question that is bound to occur to us. From what we have just read it could be argued that God is very arbitrary and unfair. But one thing must be said: God is never unfair. We can be certain that God will treat everyone with perfect justice. His perfect nature guarantees this. So what he will do with people who have never heard that Jesus is the only way is for him to decide and not for us to argue about. But we have some clues.

God has set us in a world which shows evident traces of his design, his beauty and his order. He has also created each of us with a conscience, which rings bells when we do what we know to be wrong or fail to do right. We cannot ever live up to our own standards, let alone God's. Forgiveness for our failure and power to do right can come only through the death and resurrection of Jesus.

> However, this does not necessarily mean that an individual needs to be aware of this action on his behalf, to receive its benefit. For example, when slavery was abolished in the British Empire in 1833,

thousands of men and women in Africa were made safe from the threat of abduction and captivity. Many of them knew nothing about the British Government and even less about the act of Parliament which guaranteed their freedom! Despite this ignorance, they enjoyed the freedom the act obtained for them. Any person anywhere who is really sorry for the wrong in their lives and throws themselves completely on God's mercy for their salvation can enjoy the benefits of the Christian message, even without knowing the facts about the death and resurrection of Jesus.

(From *It makes Sense* by Stephen Gaukroger, published by Scripture Union and quoted by permission.)

Chapter 12

Family likeness

Jesus said:

> *'If you really knew me, you would know my Father as well. From now on, you do know him and have him.'*
>
> *Philip said, 'Lord, show us the Father and that will be enough for us.'*
>
> *Jesus answered: 'Don't you know me, Philip, even after I have been among you such a long time? Anyone who has seen me has seen the Father.'*
>
> (John 14:7–9)

Father and Son

This was a very remarkable thing for Jesus to say, since he was talking to a group of first-century Jews. The Jews had great reverence for God, so much so that they weren't even allowed to mention his name, *Yahweh*. But here was Jesus saying, 'If you want to know what God is like, look at me.' Jesus could only say this because he himself was the Son of God and so possessed all the attributes of God. He was saying that the disciples did not need to see God, because in being with Jesus for three years they had been in God's presence all the time. There is a family likeness between God and Jesus: God is the Father, and the Son has all the characteristics of the Father.

This is what makes Christianity unique among the

world religions. All the other religions talk about God as someone who is far away, a God who is unimaginably powerful, who sees everything and everyone, a God who brought the universe into being by his will and who sustains it by his power, a God who is far too holy to approach and far too mysterious to understand. Christianity has that view of God too, but that is only half the story; the other half is that in Jesus God became a human being and lived among us. Even though he was a man Jesus possessed all the character traits of his heavenly Father. So if we want to know what God is like, we can look at Jesus to find out. To know God we don't need to be theologians or philosophers: we need only to get to know Jesus. If we want to know how God behaves, we need only to read the gospels and see how Jesus behaved, because Jesus the Son does what God the Father does.

Some people have trouble in trusting God. How can we be sure that he is trustworthy? How can we be sure that he will keep his promises? When he says he will forgive us, how can we be sure that he won't change his mind and hold all our sins against us? We have only to look at the life of Jesus. He was always completely trustworthy; he never let his friends down. When he forgave (which was all the time), he really forgave. His love was real and genuine and selfless. If that was what Jesus was like, we know that that is what God is like too.

Spiritual role models

So Jesus imitated the behaviour of his Father. He said,

'I tell you the truth, the Son can do nothing by himself; he can do only what he sees his Father doing, because whatever the Father does the Son also does.'

(John 5:19)

This has major implications for mature Christians today. Just as Jesus based his behaviour on the behaviour of his Father, so immature, baby Christians will imitate the behaviour of mature Christians. Spiritually the mature are fathers and mothers, and new Christians are their children. Mature Christians have a great responsibility to be good role models. Ideally, new Christians should model themselves only on Jesus, but in practice they will also look to other Christians for guidance on how to behave. Their understanding of the faith is as yet limited, so as far as they know the mature Christians around them are examples of what a Christian is supposed to be like. This means that the onus is on the mature Christians to be people of integrity, to live in a way which is in line with what they say. If they contradict their words by their behaviour, young Christians will become confused.

So young Christians will inevitably try to imitate us, but we should try to focus their attention away from ourselves and towards Jesus, because his life always matched his words, whereas we often fail. Sooner or later we will do something which is out of line with the faith we profess, and if the young Christians have put too much faith in us they will be disillusioned.

Of course, the same principle applies to our physical children. To a great extent they model their attitudes and behaviour on those of their parents. That does not mean that every wrong thing our children do is our fault. They are independent human beings with wills of their own. But if our children do grow up with problems, it will be at least partly our fault. For example, if a son sees his father mistreat his mother, that experience is likely to influence the way in which he will eventually treat his own wife. Children desperately need to see integrity in the lives of their parents. They need to see that the things we do are in line with the things we believe. Parents who send their children to Sunday School but never come to church themselves are an example of life not being in line with belief. The parents say to the children, 'We want you to go to Sunday School because it's really important that you learn all about Jesus and how to live as a Christian.' But the parents' own lack of commitment to Christ contradicts what they say to their children, and eventually the children realize this. The message they get is that going to Sunday School is something they have to do until they are old enough to make up their own minds about Christianity, and they will probably decide not to bother with it any more because their parents' lack of Christian commitment has convinced them that church is not important. It is perhaps better to send them, so that they have something to make up their minds about, than not to send them at all, but this is a poor second best.

We parents have to remember that our children are watching everything we do. They are absorbing our attitudes and behaviour unconsciously most of the time. We need to make sure that one of the things they do not learn from us is hypocrisy. Too many Christian children are taught by example that Christians can live in super-spiritual mode on Sundays and live in worldly mode from Monday to Saturday. They see their parents exhibiting a Christian behaviour-pattern on Sunday and a sub-Christian behaviour pattern the rest of the week. Sadly, many young people growing up in Christian homes have hypocrisy written into their experience from a very early age. Mum and Dad say God is important to them, but six days out of seven there is precious little evidence of that. I don't write all this to make my fellow parents feel guilty, but just to show the need for integrity in our homes. We need to pray that the way we talk and live will encourage our children in their Christian faith rather than discourage them.

It's not what you know but who you know

'Believe me when I say that I am in the Father and the Father is in me; or at least believe on the evidence of the miracles themselves. I tell you the truth, anyone who has faith in me will do what I have been doing. He will do even greater things than these, because I am going to the Father. And I will do whatever you ask in my name, so that the Son may bring glory to the Father. You may ask me for anything in my name, and I will do it.'

(John 14:11–14)

I would love to spend a year studying these verses and really trying to get to grips with them, because I have no idea what they mean! Moreover, I don't know anyone else who really knows what they mean. I can explain the Greek words in the original text, I can understand the tenses that are used, and I can say in principle what I think John meant here, but as to what these verses really mean *in practice*, I am at a loss. What Jesus is saying here is so profound and amazing and earth-shattering that if a church really understood it and actually had the truth of it expressed in their individual and corporate life, the results would be revolutionary. Jesus said that we can do even greater things than he did – that's mind-blowing!

People often say that it's not *what* you know that counts but *who* you know. That was certainly the case with Jesus. He was not a scholar or theologian. He had not been to any of the great centres of academic learning in the ancient world. What gave him his power and authority was his relationship with God. He didn't know as much as some of the great scholars of his day, *but he knew God*, and that relationship was of far greater value and importance than any amount of academic knowledge.

Too many of our clergy today are made less effective for God than they might be by their theological education. They have become so concerned about the jots and tittles of Scripture that they have forgotten how really to communicate the biblical message. I am not knocking theology as such: without it our churches would be much poorer spiritually, but too often the emphasis of theology is on the details of Scripture rather than its vital principles. Ultimately what you know is only of secondary importance; what matters most is who you know. Someone who knows God but has no theological knowledge can preach the gospel far better than someone who has ten theology degrees but does not have a living relationship with Jesus. What matters is not how much knowledge we have acquired, but whether or not we are in relationship with the God who can supply everything – peace, wisdom, power, patience, all the fruit of the Spirit and the gifts of the Spirit. Jesus had that relationship with God. God was his Father and he was the Son, and so Jesus was connected to the source of all power and knowledge. Because of this his ministry was characterized by miracles and by answers to prayer.

Greater things than even Jesus did!

We find it easy to accept that Jesus would have such a clear manifestation of God's power in his life because, after all, he was the Son of God. The challenging part for us is where Jesus says,

'anyone who has faith in me will do what I have been doing. He will do even greater things than these ... '

This means firstly that Jesus' followers will bring far more people into the Kingdom of God than he did, simply because Jesus had a very limited three-year period in which to do his evangelizing, and the church has had the best part of 2,000 years. It would be easy if this were all that the passage was referring to. But it surely means more than evangelism and conversion: it also includes the miraculous, such as healing, deliverance, raising the dead and so on. Jesus did all of these things, and he says that the church *will do even greater things than these'*! If this passage were only talking about converting people, then we would be off the hook, as it were: people are being converted in our churches all the time. But the passage is talking about the miraculous too, and that poses a problem for us today, because we don't see much evidence of the miraculous in our churches. We don't seem to have the sort of miracles which Jesus himself did, let alone even greater ones. Why is this? I wish I knew the full answer to that question! Perhaps we are too concerned about *what* we know and not quite aware of *who* we know: perhaps we have not really tapped into the power in that Father–Son relationship which Jesus had. As I said, I don't fully understand this passage but there does seem to be a miraculous aspect to what we are doing for Jesus as well as the scope of evangelism.

Jesus said. *'You may ask me for anything in my name, and I will do it.'* Praying for something in Jesus' name means a lot more than just tacking the words, 'In Jesus' name' onto the end of our prayers. To pray in the name of Jesus means, first of all, praying in the light of what Jesus has accomplished for us on the cross. His death made a bridge between God and mankind, and as a result God will now hear and answer our prayers. Without the cross our prayers will get no further than the ceiling. By Jesus' death we have been saved and we have a right of access into the presence of the Father. Praying in the name of Jesus means, secondly, praying in line with his authority and will. In order to pray according to his will we need to know what his will is, and sometimes that means stopping and listening to Jesus instead of just asking God to do what seems best to us.

When Christians get disappointed about their

prayers apparently not being answered, it may be because they have not really understood what it really means to pray in the name of Jesus. It is far more than a mere phrase at the end of a prayer request; it is all about a relationship with God. Jesus' prayers were always answered because he had such a close relationship with his Father, and because of that he always knew what his Father's will was in any situation. I would like the same to be true of me, but I have to confess that sometimes I am so out of step with what God wants that he answers my prayers with a 'No'. I get out of step with him because I have not spent enough time listening to him.

So John 14:11–14 remain something of a mystery. How can we see *greater things than these* happening in our churches? As I said I'm not sure what the answer is. But I do know one thing: a slick, easy answer to this issue is bound to be the wrong answer. The manifestation of the miraculous in our churches which Jesus is talking about here is not something which can be had cheaply: it will require the commitment of our whole lives. It will not come about through a neat theological principle or a clever spiritual technique. An essential part of that total commitment is the *desire* to see God work amongst us in miraculous power. This is not for the curiosity value of miracles but so that God will be glorified and the Kingdom of God may be manifested in authority as it was in the gospels and in Acts. I believe that when enough people in a church yearn sincerely enough for that miraculous dimension to be seen, then miracles will begin to happen – perhaps little ones at first, but getting bigger as people's faith and yearning grows. Some people in the church will at first respond with cynicism, thinking that it is all just coincidence and emotionalism, but when the miracles keep happening they will discard their cynicism and believe it.

The work of the Holy Spirit

Jesus said, *'If you love me, you will obey what I command'* (verse 15). We can talk about loving God as much as we want; we can stand with our eyes closed and our hands raised during worship, telling him we love him, but that won't be worth a scrap to God unless we are also prepared to be obedient to him. Obedience is the acid test of our love for God.

Jesus promised the disciples,

'I will ask the Father, and he will send you another Counsellor to be with you for ever …'

(verse 16)

the Holy Spirit. The Greek word which the NIV translates as 'Counsellor' is *paraklētos* which literally means one who is called alongside to help. The old King James Version used the word 'Comforter', which when the translation was made meant someone who gave strength, but today the word 'Comforter' suggests someone who sympathizes, which is not all that the Greek text means. The NIV's 'Counsellor' is more accurate and helpful.

What does the Holy Spirit do in our lives? Several of his roles are mentioned in this passage by Jesus. First, as we have already seen, he is our Counsellor or adviser. He longs to give us advice. Secondly, he is *the Spirit of truth* (verse 17). He longs to guide us into truth and away from error. He is never, ever wrong. He gives us his advice and truth through three main means: the advice of mature Christians, the Word of God and prayer. If we seek his advice through all three of those means, not neglecting any of them, the Holy Spirit will speak to us through them and we will not wander into error and mistakes. (I have noticed that when Christians make a bad decision it is usually because, having prayed about the matter and searched in the Word about it, they then don't bother to talk to a mature Christian about it. Having missed out on some good advice, they then make a bad decision.)

Thirdly, the Spirit teaches us:

'the Counsellor, the Holy Spirit, whom the Father will send in my name, will teach you all things ...'

(verse 26)

He explains the Word of God to us, helping us to understand it and apply it to our lives. Fourthly, the Spirit is a reminder:

'the Holy Spirit ... will remind you of everything I have said to you.'

(verse 26)

He constantly reminds us of things God has taught us in the past. Often, in moments of need he will remind us of a Scripture verse, or some valuable thing we learned in a Christian book or a sermon. In this capacity he acts like the prompter in a play. We are the actors on the stage, and even before we forget our lines he tells us what to say. However, he can only remind us of things we already know, so that's why we need to memorize Scripture verses and learn all we can about God and his Word.

Jesus said, *'you know him, for he lives with you and will be in you'* (verse 17). So fifthly, the Holy Spirit lives within us. The implications of that are immense. And finally, he is the *Holy* Spirit. He is the Holy God, and he cannot abide sin and impurity. So we need to be careful not to grieve him by sin in our lives. If we have all sorts of wonderful spiritual experiences but our lives are not holy, those experiences are of little value; the chief work of the Holy Spirit within us is to make us more holy, more like Jesus.

The Word for the World

Growing with John's Gospel (Book 1)

STEPHEN GAUKROGER

One of the most influential books ever written was the Gospel of John.

Here we encounter at first hand the truths of Jesus. Stephen Gaukroger explains in down-to-earth language the foundations of the Christian faith as revealed in this Gospel. In it he:

- shows us Jesus – the Word of God for the world
- explains the wonders of 'the new birth'
- motivates us to be disciples
- examines the radical signs and wonders of Jesus

All come vividly to life today.

This volume, covering chapters 1 to 6 of John's Gospel, is the first in a three-volume series.

Stephen Gaukroger, recently President of the Baptist Union of Great Britain, is a widely respected Bible teacher and conference speaker. The author of many books, he is a series editor for the Crossway Bible Guides and has written Acts in that series. He and his wife Janet have three children and live in Luton, England.

117 pages *'B' format*

Crossway Books